MW00535364

A WOMAN'S

Journey

TO BECOMING

Mother 2 Many

A WOMAN'S

Journey

TO BECOMING

Mother 2 Many

JOANN WITTLER

**REDEMPTION
PRESS**

© 2022 by Joann Wittler. All rights reserved.

Published by Redemption Press, PO Box 427, Enumclaw, WA 98022.
Toll-Free (844) 2REDEEM (273-3336)

Redemption Press is honored to present this title in partnership with the author. The views expressed or implied in this work are those of the author. Redemption Press provides our imprint seal representing design excellence, creative content, and high-quality production.

The author has tried to recreate events, locales, and conversations from memories of them. In order to maintain their anonymity, in some instances the names of individuals, some identifying characteristics, and some details may have been changed, such as physical properties, occupations, and places of residence.

Noncommercial interests may reproduce portions of this book without the express written permission of the author, provided the text does not exceed five hundred words. When reproducing text from this book, include the following credit line: *"A Woman's Journey to Becoming Mother 2 Many* by Joann Wittler. Used by permission."

Commercial interests: No part of this publication may be reproduced in any form, stored in a retrieval system, or transmitted in any form by any means—electronic, photocopy, recording, or otherwise—without prior written permission of the publisher/author, except as provided by United States of America copyright law.

Author has permission to quote all emails used in the story.

Unless otherwise indicated, all Scripture quotations are from the Holy Bible, New International Version®, NIV®. Copyright © 1973, 1978, 1984, 2011 by Biblica, Inc.™ Used by permission of Zondervan. All rights reserved worldwide. www.zondervan.com. The "NIV" and "New International Version" are trademarks registered in the United States Patent and Trademark Office by Biblica, Inc.™

Scripture quotations marked (NKJV) are from the New King James Version®. Copyright © 1982 by Thomas Nelson. Used by permission. All rights reserved.

Scripture quotations marked (ESV) are from The ESV® Bible (The Holy Bible, English Standard Version®), copyright © 2001 by Crossway, a publishing ministry of Good News Publishers. Used by permission. All rights reserved.

Author bio photo provided by Janna Slaback

ISBN 13: 978-1-64645-271-2 (Paperback)
978-1-64645-272-9 (ePub)
978-1-64645-273-6 (Mobi)

Library of Congress Catalog Card Number: 2022915571

Contents

INTRODUCTION

Everyone has a story, and I want to share mine, a story to encourage you, to give you hope, and to help you trust in a God that will never fail you nor ever leave you. It was 2013, and I was fifty-three when I was called into ministry. Some might think, *It is too late, I am too old*, but God said it was just in time.

My name is Joann. I was born in Washington state and have lived there for most of my life. I love family, trips, the sun—yeah, I know I am in the wrong state for that—football, volleyball, and nice walks in the woods. I enjoy writing and my time in our outreach ministry. Children have always had my heart, even when at times I did not see it. I have been married to Steven for thirty-eight years and have raised four wonderful children Jeremy, Joshua, and Stefani, and Jason my stepson. I now am a grandmother to five amazing grandchildren: Keyland, Natalie, Danika, Jeslyn, and Hayden.

My life's journey has brought me to an amazing time in my life. As I look back from the time I was little to where I am now, I see that God was preparing me for a time such as this. He was preparing me to help His children who are forgotten, alone, and wondering if anyone cares. He gave me an outreach that is truly one of a kind, and it is my honor to share with you what God has done.

Was my journey unique? I imagine we all ponder this question from time to time. I often wonder what is it that God saw in Steve and me that made Him say, *I want them to run a skate park outreach and for Joann to be a mother to many.* He saw my heart, and then He opened my eyes to see all the times He was right there with me when I felt alone and forgotten. And He saw me saying yes to Him when many might have said no. I'm hoping that you can see yourself in my story, to help you say yes too.

We are never too old to do what God has called us to do. Along with my husband, it was my time to step out and do something totally out of our comfort zone, something we really knew nothing about, but God said I want you to do this for me. The Holy Spirit became my teacher and encourager. He made sure that when I thought I could not do this, He said, *Oh yes, you can*.

Come alongside me and see what God can do in an ordinary woman's life and how He has been preparing me since I was a little girl to become a mother to many. My story as you read it may look just like yours, and that is my hope, to allow you to see that if you say yes to God, He can do the impossible, and your life will never be the same. Our God is an amazing God and when we say yes, a whole new door opens, and you, too, will become the person that God intended you to be! For me it was truly becoming a mother to many.

CHAPTER 1

Saying Yes to God Is the Biggest Step You Will Ever Make

Come to me, all you who are weary and burdened, and I will give you rest. Take my yoke upon you and learn from me, for I am gentle and humble in heart, and you will find rest for your souls.

Matthew 11:28

On January 1, 2013, our church pastor asked us to do a forty-day fast. As I listened to his words, my spirit told me, *God has something for you.* For the past three months, God had been birthing something in me. I could feel it. The feeling was one of anticipation for something wonderful, almost the same feeling of being pregnant, excited to hold my baby that I knew was nine months away. As if my body was still getting ready for the big day when I would get to meet the little one I had been carrying for nine months, God was birthing a ministry in me, and it, too, would take some time before it was ready to come out.

With great anticipation I decided to do the fast. Although I had never done a fast before, after hearing those words, I knew this was the way to truly hear what God was saying. This was exciting because I knew in my heart that something great was going to come of this. I was not disappointed. For my fast I decided to give up sweets. I have a terrible sweet tooth, so I decided to give up chocolate. I am glad that I did the fast because it changed my life forever.

As the forty days were passing, I was worshiping at church one Sunday morning and heard God's voice, crystal clear, say to me, *You will be the mother to many.* I did not understand what this meant, the mother to many. Was God going to give me a lot of kids or have me run a foster home? My mind was whirling with a ton of questions. first, I had my doubts and fears. I thought, *Lord, I've raised four children, but I do not know how to raise children that are not my own, and especially not a lot of them. What is it you really want me to do?* The fear was of the unknown, not knowing exactly what God wanted me to do as a mother to many.

I waited, not wanting to jump into anything. Being patient is not my strong suit, and God waited a week before He told me the rest. I heard these words again at church. I was to help youth who were experiencing homelessness. I had no idea what I was to do with that. My mind was going crazy with all kinds of thoughts. *Homeless teens—what does that look like? Do I move them into my home? Do I start a home? What do you want me to do, Lord?*

I've never worked with homeless teens, and I knew nothing, but God was going to show me, and He was going to teach me all I needed to know. My life was about to change in my way of thinking and feeling and my understanding of what homelessness was all about. At first, I did not even tell my husband, I just could not believe God wanted me to be a mother to many.

God's Word tells us:

> The Spirit of the Lord is on me. He has put his hand on me to preach the good news to poor people. He has sent me to heal those with a sad heart. He has sent me to tell those who are being held that they can go free. He has sent me to make the blind to see and to free those who are held because of trouble. (Luke 4:18)

As I read this Scripture, it came to life for me. It was all I needed to tell God I am all in and ask what He wanted me to do. And this is where Mother 2 Many came to life. The name became who I was to become. Let me explain what the phrase "mother to many" means by breaking down each word for understanding. A *mother* is someone who is nurturing, who loves unconditionally, and who will always be there in the good times and bad times. In the spiritual sense, the number *two* reminds us of the power if two or more agree in God's name. Two is a number that can be so many things, but God points out the number two as being very important in our ministry. Always two people out at the parks, with two people in prayer, all things are possible, two are safer than one. *Many* suggests there is no limit to how many youths we would help.

How was I going to help the youth? This was something God was going to have to tell me. I had no idea; I just knew He wanted me to work with them. My heart was telling me, *I am supposed to be there for youth who need to know they matter; I am supposed to be a mother figure, someone they could count on, someone they can look up to.*

Also, in helping youth, what was God asking me to do? My first thought was to house them, feed them, clothe them, and help them know they were not alone. In time I would find out exactly what God wanted us to do, and yes, we were to do all those things, but not the way we were thinking.

Two weeks after the fast ended, my pastor shared a sermon on the promises of God and whether we are willing to accept what He had for us. He asked for anyone who wanted to accept what God had for them to raise their hand. My hand shot right up without a thought, as if the Holy Spirit did it for me. This amazed me. When I walked to the front, there were two people that I had been heading toward for prayer. Others got there first, so I went to another couple instead. In the next moment, I would discover that God had this couple chosen specifically for me.

When I asked them to pray, I cried, then said, "I don't know what God wants of me, but I will do it."

The husband, Gary, had a word for me. "A giant redwood has many roots, and those roots are people that God is preparing to use or assist you on the journey God has for you."

Before Gary's prayer, I was still in denial because I was afraid, even though his word was confirmation of what I needed to do. I needed to share my vision with my husband, Steve. I did, and I was surprised that he was OK with it. I was worried to share with him; I thought he might think I was crazy or something like that. Instead of rejecting my ideas as I had initially feared, Steve told me, "If God is telling you to do this, then I will support whatever He says."

It was one of the kindest things my husband has ever done for me and was further confirmation God was preparing me, my husband, and others for something wonderful. Satan likes to put doubt and fear into us that our spouses or family might not be accepting of the word. The enemy will try to make us doubt ourselves, that we can't do this, we have no idea what we are doing, but then God will bring up a song or bring a friend or even a word from a devotional that will remind us that we are going to be OK because He is right here with us. God is always the winner and will always bring us encouragement to move forward.

When God told me I would be working with homeless teens, I could not believe that He wanted me to work with the very age group I disliked! I was a little confused here. I raised four teens, including one from my husband's previous marriage. Teens could be hard to work with. They are mouthy, rude, and give those looks when they think what you're saying is dumb, like rolling the eyes or a very long sigh. God has a great sense of humor. He was going to show me a side that I didn't see in my own children because I was not the teens' mom, but I was a mother figure, which is totally different in how other youth treat you.

Over the next six years, God would teach me, remake me, and give me a love for youth I never thought I could have. He broke down walls I didn't realize I had. He healed hurts I thought would never be healed. He taught me that my heart was bigger than I thought it could ever be, and He showed me I could love like He loves. All because I said yes. And I know that by obeying and having faith in Him I was given a heart to love these young people.

God never gives you anything He doesn't think you can handle, so I decided to let Him lead the way with my husband and me as the vessels. God would also teach me to overcome those fears I had with the youth who did not have parents to love or care for them. One of the fears I had was not knowing what I was doing, which I thought was odd. I guess this was different; it was other people's kids. God saw something in me, and He believed in me, so I needed to do the same. Thinking of what these teens needed and letting God lead and guide me would change my outlook on teenagers.

God gave me specifics for what I needed to do to win the youth over. One is the most important: Be consistent. Too many youths have had too many adults make broken promises. In contrast, being consistent lets them know you genuinely care. Never tell them you are going to do something and then not follow through. For example, if you tell one of them you are going to bring them a hat next week, you had better have that hat next week. Once they know you are for real, you will see kind, thankful, loving youth. Since we were going to deal with youth who were hungry for love and acceptance and, most of all, for adults who had time to listen to them and hear their hearts, listening and hearing were important rules to follow.

Dealing with youth who have been hurt can be the hardest. They will seem shut off from everything and everyone. They will seem disrespectful, but these are usually the youth that have been hurt the worst. They will use behavior, words, or actions to keep you from getting too close, and this, too, is just a way of protecting themselves. This is the time you never give up; they need to know you are for real and not just a fly-by-night person in their lives. Consistency is the key word here; do not give up.

Once they saw that we were not going anywhere, the youth we saw every week were totally different. They were incredibly grateful and genuinely nice to talk with. They made us laugh and smile, and we did the same for them. God would also teach me that *just because a youth has a home, doesn't mean they are not homeless*, as this was the type of youth we were working with. He would teach me that not everyone chooses to be homeless, that life can be very cruel to some, and a teen's only way out is to leave home or to look to others for a family or some kind of community connection.

Before I share how God really worked out the past six years of being a mother to many, I must first share a bit about my childhood adventures with you because it truly is amazing how God works in each of us to bring about His purpose and plan for our lives. God's plan for me didn't start at fifty-three, it truly started right at the beginning of my life.

Lord, I come to You in prayer, asking that You guide me, direct me, and open my eyes to see what You have for me to do. Let my yes be yes. Do not let fear take over, because I know You will not put me on the journey alone. You are with me always. In Jesus's name, amen.

CHAPTER 2

My Beginning: God Had a Plan from the Start

"Because he loves me," says the Lord, "I will rescue him;
I will protect him, for he acknowledges my name. He will
call on me, and I will answer him; I will be with him
in trouble, I will deliver him and honor him, With long
life I will satisfy him and show him my salvation."

Psalm 91:14–16

In August 1960, God brought me into this world, a child who was a surprise to my parents but not to Him. I am the oldest of five children, the oldest grandchild on my dad's side, and the oldest granddaughter on my mom's side. That will give you an idea of my personality. I am independent and a leader. People have always depended on me and still do to this day.

Now being a strong girl and woman, it is sad to say, there are people who go out of their way to hurt you, and people I have trusted or thought were family have gone out of their way to hurt me the most. Because of that, I have held so much rejection, heartbreak, and mistrust that have caused me more hurt. I also have felt much abandonment from people I love and care for and am fond of. Because of that rejection, my path went in a direction that was not good. It was very lonely and destructive in many ways. But it did not start that way. God was trying to lead me down a path I was supposed to take, but the Enemy had other plans. God gives us choices, and at first, I made good choices. But then I started to make wrong ones—I let my emotions and insecurities get in the way.

The Lord has a plan for all of us once we are placed on this earth. Our adversary, Satan, does everything possible to keep that plan from happening. The enemy does not know God's plan, but he has an idea, and once he has a sniff, he is out there to see who he can take down. Thank goodness our God has got this and is much bigger than what could ever assail us. We understand He has already won the war.

My prayer for you is:

Heavenly Father, I come to You and ask that You give me strength to do what You have called me to do. I ask that You give me knowledge, wisdom, and ears to hear You clearly. I ask that if the reader of this book is being called, that You will help them see they are not alone, that You are with them always. And because You have called them, they will succeed. Amen.

I was just two years old when Satan first tried to stop God's plan for me. My parents and I and my siblings lived in an area where people did not lock their doors. We did not have to worry about people trying to break in. I was an overly active two-year-old and decided to visit my neighbor's house with my little sister, Kathy. They were at work, and back in the early sixties no one locked their doors, so it was easy for us to sneak in. My mom was unaware that her two little girls were no longer playing outside but checking out the neighbor's kitchen. They had many interesting cupboards that piqued our interest. We pulled up a chair to see what was on the upper shelves and found some interesting looking "candy." By the time our mother found us, it was too late. We had eaten our neighbor's medications.

We were whisked off to the emergency room, where the last thing I remember was a plastic tube coming toward my face and the nurse telling me everything would be OK. When having your stomach pumped, they put a very long tube through your nose and into your stomach to get out anything that is not supposed to be there. Almost like a vacuum cleaner, it will suck out what it is supposed to get. My mother said she could hear the two of us screaming throughout the hospital while we had our stomachs pumped. Because this hospital was old with high ceilings, our screams echoed through the hall. They were able to remove the drugs from my sister's stomach, but not mine. My parents were told to keep watch on me throughout the night because if the pills did not dissolve the right way, I could die.

Almighty God had plans for me. I lived, and here I am, writing my story today. While the devil has made many more attempts to take my life, God has always been there to make sure he did not succeed.

At the age of four, I went to church with my grandmother. But when I got older, it was off and on with her, so I would ride my bicycle the six blocks to church. I remember loving the Sunday school teacher because she was always nice and welcoming. Due to my dad's work schedule and my mom raising five children mostly on her own, as the oldest, I felt my needs were always put on the back burner. I found myself gravitating toward older women to fill that void of motherly attention. Thank goodness the women I did go to were good strong godly women who had a big impact in my life. I still think kindly of them to this day.

While I had good relationships with the women in my life, my relationships with the men in my life were not as good. The relationship with my dad was not the best. He tried, always making sure we had nice gifts for Christmas, the pair of shoes we loved for school, and our yearbooks. I was able to play sports, which entailed physicals each year, but he didn't really know how to raise daughters. He didn't realize as a dad to girls that we needed those daddy hugs, and we needed to know that we were loved. Because he didn't realize this, as I got older, I started to look for attention from the opposite sex.

I remember when I was in sixth grade, my grandma telling me, "You were so cute when you were little." This is not something a young girl needed to hear, and even after all these years, I can still hear those words. Once I was in junior high, things started to change for me concerning men, or rather, boys. The boys thought I was cute, and I realized I was not ugly after all. I would become so needy that I usually chased them away. They must have thought I was weird or just plain clingy. Not a confidence booster to be rejected at a young age by boys you thought were cute, that is for sure.

Just like the empty father-daughter relationship I had with my earthly father, my view of God fit similarly. I had no clue of the true relationship I could have with God. When I was thirteen and in eighth grade, we started attending church regularly, which was good because my walk with God began to grow. Even when I was younger, I would talk to God, desiring His presence with me always. But because my relationship with my earthly father was not good, I didn't quite understand the kind of relationship I could have with my heavenly Father.

I wish so much I would have known back then what I know now because I could have gotten past so much heartache in my life. Yet if not for my past, I would not be where I am today. Without those experiences, I would not be able to minister and care for those who feel abandoned and forgotten today. God is not a religion but a relationship. God was going to change all that for me. He longs to have a relationship with each of us. It would take me until I was in my fifties to utterly understand and accept the relationship He was offering.

Growing up, my relationship with my dad had never been a touchy-feely, hugging type, and that was something I truly longed for as a young girl. My grandparents, aunts, and uncles were all very loving, which helped fill a small gap, but it is not the same as a daddy's love and attention. Through my high school years, I stayed active in church. I was a camp counselor and involved in Young Life but still had that father love missing part in my life.

Thankfully, I had few boyfriends and stayed a virgin the entire time I was in high school. This is surprising because I had wanted to feel loved and accepted, and with my personality and athletic body I had the tools to get just that, but that would have left me empty too.

When I finally graduated from high school in 1978, I was without any real plan for my future. I had wanted to be a cop, but God kept closing that door. I would pass one test but then not the other. I became an explorer for the local police department and learned a lot about law enforcement. I learned I could correct a person in authority but making sure I was respectful. I used this as an explorer—and then later when I became mother to many. When youth would take a water bottle and throw it up in the air to see if it landed right, I would have to show authority so the kids would listen and not be disrespectful of items that people donated, but would not hate me because I was giving them boundaries.

In the meantime, as I was trying to figure out what I was to do, I worked at a restaurant as a waitress (being an explorer was a volunteer position). Here is where I thought I had met the love of my life. A man, who was tall, dark, and handsome frequented the restaurant. He was a police officer like my dad, although my dad was *short*, dark, and handsome. Watching this tall policeman and waiting his table, I thought maybe he was someone I could get to know better. I thought he had all the qualities of a man I was hoping to be with, and his being a police officer was very appealing to me. I guess in some ways I was seeing things in him that I felt I needed in my life and was blinded by my needs and wants.

After about three months, he asked me out. He came over to the place where I was babysitting, and suddenly my life took a terrible turn. We did not go all the way, but things happened, and I was hooked to a man who turned my world upside down.

A week later I remember going to his house and knocking on the door, only to have a woman answer. When I had asked who she was, she responded that she was the girlfriend of the man I went to see. What a shock to the system. A young woman thinking intelligently probably would have said, *I'm out of here*, but not me. She went and got him, and he didn't look too happy when he came to the door. She was not with him, so he asked me to come back later, which I did. Guess what? We slept together, thus I lost my virginity and was now madly in lust with this man. This man who had a live-in girlfriend!

I was eighteen, and he was twenty-four. We saw each other off and on for four years.

When we would break up, I would find a new guy. There was always sex involved. I wanted a man's love, and my body became the tool for how I got it. I was very athletic, had a toned figure, and looked cute. I've always been very outgoing and could befriend most people. There was never a problem getting willing men; however, the ones I wanted would not commit, and the ones who did were not my type.

As I grew up and looked back on the full picture, I realized my tall, dark, and handsome policeman boyfriend went after young naïve girls (later even marrying one of them). The enemy was doing everything possible to destroy my life. He was bringing me down to the lowest possible point. But through all this, God was still there, He protected me. I never got pregnant, though one would imagine I should have had many children, but God knew that I would start down a better path.

After two years of ups and down with my boyfriend, we broke up, I had caught him in bed with another woman—surprise, not really. People tried to tell me; I just didn't listen. After six months we were seeing each other again for a time, but nothing serious. Then one day came when my policeman boyfriend had once again popped into the picture, and we were seeing each other more. He was single now, and I was right there for him.

As I look back, it was the movie *Groundhog Day*, and I just kept repeating the same mistake over and over again. Not a wise move on my part, but God was there, and He was going to make sure we were really done. He had to go out of state to visit his mom and was gone for three weeks. This was the opportunity God was waiting for. My boyfriend needed to be out of my life because if he wasn't, I was literally at his beck and call. When he called, I was there and in love, or so I thought.

One weekend a friend of mine and I decided to go to Alki Beach to hang out. I was a big volleyball player, and some guys were playing beach volleyball. We asked to play, and they said no, so we decided to sit in the sand and watch them play. Shortly after, a young man came over and asked if we still wanted to play, and I happily said yes. My friend did not know how to play, and I found out beach volleyball was hard; it was not like court playing.

We all played a few games, then sat down on the beach. One of the guys, who had been genuinely nice came over to sit by me. His name was Steve. We talked all day. He was wonderful. He told me he had a son.

Oh my gosh. He is married. It had seemed a lot of men I had been meeting were married, and I was thinking this was the only type of men I could meet. Thankfully I learned he had been divorced for three years. Soon it was time to leave, and we said our goodbyes. But Steve didn't ask me for my number.

I was sad because I thought I finally met a really nice guy, and he didn't want my number.

"No, you don't ask him," my friend said, pulling me toward our vehicle.

We were almost to the car when he came running over, asking for my number. Two days later we talked on the phone, all night in fact! I worked the graveyard shift as a hotel operator, which created the perfect opportunity to talk. Before we talked that night, Steve had gone to a class reunion with another woman he had been seeing off and on for a few years. At the end of the date, he said he was done. He was at the point in his life that he knew he needed to make some changes. He thought us talking could be a step toward those changes by furthering our relationship. It was the beginning of a new relationship for two people at the same point in their lives, looking toward new directions, both of us wanting to do what we thought God wanted us to do.

The next weekend I traveled to Canada, and Steve joined me on the second day. I went home with him. We had sex, but this time around, I found out I was pregnant four weeks later. We were both scared but knew that, even though our courtship was short, we wanted to be together.

Even though we did not start things off in alignment with God's Word, I knew this was the man I was supposed to marry. Thankfully Steve felt the same. My life had been spiraling, and Steve was the one who brought me back up. He was part of God's plan for my life, and I'm so very glad I was listening. We met August 18, 1982, and married October 29, 1982. It was fast, but we both knew we were the one for each other. Plus, I was pregnant. Steven was the husband God had shown me long ago in my dreams. He is my greatest blessing and has shown me what a man's love truly is—my Steven.

After eight years of marriage and three children and one stepson, we were ready to call it quits. I had fallen out of love with my husband. Even though God had put us together, we carried a lot of baggage that never got cleaned out. When I told him we had to either get counseling or a divorce, he chose counseling. Unbeknownst to me, my husband had talked to a divorce lawyer that very day.

I was young, twenty-two, when I became a wife and took on the role of a stepmom to a ten-year-old boy. I thought I could do it, and I thought I could take on having my husband being married before, but I found that road hard. I was not mature enough to take all this on—but God came in and redid our marriage.

After six months of counseling and both of us talking to a wonderful man of God, we started to grow together in the right ways. We added God into our marriage and put each other ahead of others. We put our immediate family first after that.

Our marriage was healed by the Almighty. He gave us a love for each other that was and is still amazing. God brought the love back into our marriage. We had a good marriage before, but ex-wives and in-laws can make life hard. God wanted to make our marriage great.

Because Steve and I carried a lot of baggage with us from past relationships, we had begun to compare and judge each other. After counseling, we began to heal, and we both changed. Is our marriage perfect? Heck, no; but I could never imagine my life without him in it. God had a plan for us, and no matter what, He wanted us to remain together. Now Steve and I have four wonderful children, a son-in-law, daughter-in-law, and five grandchildren.

Once our children had all moved out of the home, it was time to think about retirement. I am ten years younger than Steve and had figured I would work until my late fifties. Little did I know God had other plans for us.

My husband has been incredibly supportive in what God called me to do. Our children probably thought we were crazy, but they backed us one hundred percent. God has blessed me with an amazing family that has helped me more than I could have ever imagined in our new adventure with the Lord. And as they've seen Mom and Dad grow in the Lord, their lives have been touched, and that makes this even a bigger blessing to me.

But of course, there is much more to this part of the story. God has asked me to share the one part of my life that I kept locked away, the part of my life that I was never proud of, but one that now helps me to understand and have compassion on the youth we serve.

God had to heal me of my abandonments and my feelings of unworthiness. God had to help me see and believe that I was worthy and not abandoned. Most of all, I had to realize I was loved by my heavenly Father, and that He loved me unconditionally. I was so special to Him. I'm His sunshine, His little girl. We serve an amazing God that is always thinking about us, and just wants us to bring our pain to Him so He can take it away. Accept Him into your heart. All the angels in heaven rejoice when we do, God does a happy dance, and we are finally redeemed in a safe, loving place.

As I got older, God gave me an understanding of my dad and showed me that he loves me. My dad is my dad, and I love him. Most importantly, I have let go of that hurt, and I decided to not hold on to the past. I have moved forward, and once God had shared with me more of what my dad has gone through in life, it helped me to completely let go.

As my life has matured in Christ and I've let go and dropped most of the walls, God showed me the hurts that my dad has kept in, and those hurts are as big as mine or bigger. God replaced anger with compassion. I do not want to end my days disliking my dad but loving him just the way he is. When we get to heaven, I know my dad is going to give me the biggest hug ever and will welcome me home.

Everything in life is a lesson. We are blessed to be able to take our past and do something good with it if we choose. To glorify God with our past makes our past seem useful. Even though it is something we would like to forget, we become overcomers when we use our past for glorifying God, and I'm so thankful that if I can help one person, then I have done what I needed to do. God has shown me that He never left me, that He was always with me. He cried with me, He screamed with me, and He also was especially with me in the good parts of my life. God is so good. What an honor to serve God's children for Him.

My prayer for you is this, and again, I invite you to pray out loud:

Dear Father, thank You for loving me. Thank You for being so patient with me and for guiding me. I ask for Your wisdom as I move forward in Your will. Open doors that need to be opened and close doors that need to be closed. Bring me others who are like-minded in my journey, and guard me from those who are not. In Jesus's name, amen.

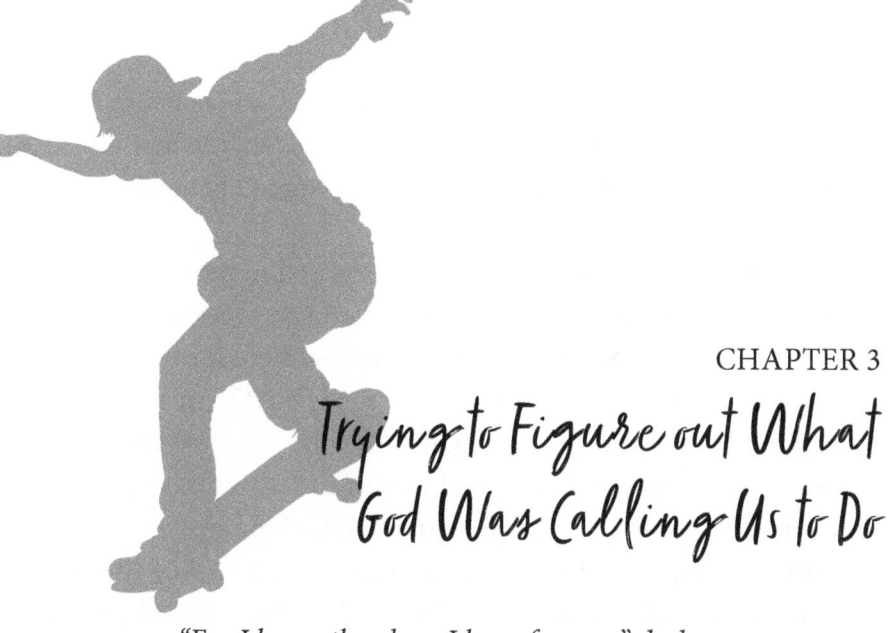

Trying to Figure out What God Was Calling Us to Do

*"For I know the plans I have for you," declares
the Lord, "plans to prosper you and not to harm
you, plans to give you hope and a future."*

Jeremiah 29:11

In January 2013, I had gotten the word that I would be a mother to many, working with homeless teens. I was still not sure what that meant. In February I shared with close friends and family what God had said, and everyone was really excited for Steve and me.

I was still working full-time at the bank, and that meant ten-hour days; that made it impossible to start doing what God wanted me to do. I shared with one of my friends what I felt God was leading me toward and that I needed to talk to people who could help me understand where God was calling me. To my excitement my friend knew a lady named Pat who worked with the homeless in Burien, Washington.

I called Pat and asked if I could meet with her. She was more than happy to do so. We met at her place of employment, an old school that had been turned into a place where people experiencing homelessness could come and get clothes, food, and even furniture. Pat was about sixty and wore a bandanna. She was the sweetest lady with a kind heart and love for the people she was helping. I liked her right from the start. I shared with her that I felt God was calling me to help homeless teens. I was to feed them, but I was not sure what else God was calling me to do. She then told me that the best way to meet homeless youth or those who do not have good home lives is at the skate park.

This piqued my interest, and I was excited to hear more. She suggested we get water and granola bars and sit around. The kids would approach us. She told me it could take time for the kids to approach because they needed to know they could trust us, and to keep going so we could build relationships with them. My time with her was a great encouragement, and what she told me about going to the skate park sounded great and stirred something in me to check into this further. I could visualize Steve and myself helping youth at skate parks, which was important for me since I'm a visual person. Pat planted a seed, even though it took time to grow.

I also had a great boss who knew a lot of people in the community. While I was trying to figure out what God wanted us to do exactly, I shared with him what I felt God wanted us to do. My boss was a man of faith, and I knew he wouldn't laugh at me for what I felt I was being led to do. Within the next week, my boss was talking to organizations that dealt with homelessness and setting up meetings. I was able to meet with people during my lunch hour. And my job was a great way of talking to my customers whom I had gotten to know well about what I was feeling called to do. I received so much encouragement that it made me want to get going faster.

One day, God started to download everything that He wanted me to gather and what I needed to get started. I had a list of dos and don'ts. One thing God impressed on my heart that has always stuck with me: just because the people you see have nothing doesn't mean they do not deserve the best. We were able to get new hats, new gloves, and nice, gently worn coats—all the items needed to be cleaned. God also gave me the people He wanted to serve with us to help us know what to get and how to get it. My first task was to ask friends and family for donations of toiletry items, coats, and later, snack items. In the first two weeks, I had enough donations to fill fifty Blessing Bags.

God also impressed upon me to put handwritten notes into the bags we were to hand out. I shared this with my brother, and to my surprise, he told me he had already been writing notes, leaving them at restaurants, at rest stops, and on grocery store shelves. He had written about a hundred more of them and would give them to me. This was great because handwritten notes were more personal than typed notes. Getting a note saying *You matter* or *You're loved* would be a great encouragement to the precious ones we would meet.

On March 14, 2013, we had a guest speaker at church. After the service Steve, and I told him what our plans were, and he looked at Steve and asked, "Are you in agreement?" Steve said yes with resounding confidence.

Then right before he prayed for us, to ask God to direct us and lead us, I said to Steve, "Are you ready?" because I knew this prayer would bring down the walls of Jericho in our lives, and we would never be the same. We were about to step into God's plan for our lives. Even though we didn't know exactly what that was yet, we knew God was going to start teaching us about homelessness and hurting youth. Best of all, God was calling us to help them.

For six months we met with a few different organizations, faith- and nonfaith-based. But I knew in time I would have more time to meet with others, but this was a start. God was helping us assemble a puzzle, and every time we met someone new or learned something new, it added a piece to that puzzle.

God even told us how to dress when we went out. Nothing flashy. Jeans, T-shirts, no heavy makeup, and no flashy jewelry. We did not want the homeless to feel like we thought we were better than them. We needed to be approachable and easy to talk with, two traits I noticed when meeting people who worked with the homeless. As God was preparing me, He also told me that there would be many tears and heartache, but there would be much joy when working with those who were hurting and felt like no one cared about them.

By the end of April 2013, we received our business license, making us officially a nonprofit. Now it was time to make things official. I turned one of our extra rooms into an office. As we arranged this room, God kept showing me the sun. And it was neat because when I had my daughter help me with the brochure, she used a sun. I love the sun; it is bright and warm, makes me smile, and makes me happy. The sun also makes others happy. Which are all the things that God does. We decided to use the sun on every M2M brochure because the sun represented Jesus, and He was the focus.

There is a meaning in everything we have and have done. We decided to paint a sun on one of the walls in my office. I was going to finish by rounding the top, but my granddaughter said, "Grandma, you need to make it all the way to the ceiling." She was so right.

After that God spoke these words to me: "Don't limit Me, Joann, for My love has no boundaries." God is so good. We will have the sun painted wherever God leads us, and the rays will go on forever, just like our heavenly Father.

At the end of April, during one of the church services, I thought more about my job situation and went up front to ask for prayer. I wanted to make sure to do what God wanted, not what I wanted to do. At the end of the prayer, one of the ladies who prayed for me told me that God wanted me to have the heart of a child.

That got me to thinking. When I was a child, I trusted God in all things, but as I grew older, I trusted less. God was nudging me once again to have more trust in Him. I believed I could do that, so I waited until God told me it was the right time to leave my job and work with M2M full-time.

One day at work, I was told to get the book, *The Cross and the Switchblade*. As I read through this book, I could relate to Pastor Wilkerson. His dad was a pastor, my dad was a cop. I know a lot of people think that kids from those types of dads were bad, but neither of us were. We did not experience the lives that the youth we were going to deal with had experienced. The pastor didn't do drugs, and I never did drugs; he knew nothing about addiction, I knew nothing about homelessness—yet God chose both of us at different times to deal with His kids. To love them, to guide them, to give them hope. God saw both hearts, and He knew we would say yes, and we wouldn't stop doing what we were called to do. God taught him and directed him, and he ended up starting Teen Challenge, an amazing organization that helps youth with addictions. The book was a great inspiration for me.

If God could help and teach David Wilkerson, I knew God could help and teach me. One interesting thing to note is that Pastor Wilkerson wanted to start right away, but the Lord closed the door many times until finally, the door opened wide, allowing Pastor Wilkerson to do great things with the youth. What I was going through was similar, and the book helped me realize that this was all part of God's plan. Not mine, but His. God was taking an unqualified person and qualifying them. I had to be patient and wait on Him because He is never early or late. He is right on time.

Dear Father, we come to You and ask for direction, Lord, help us to not go to the right or to the left, but continue to follow You. Help us to be patient and to wait on You, because amazing things happen when we wait. Thank You, Father, for choosing me! In Jesus's name, amen.

CHAPTER 4

Allowing God to Heal Those Broken Areas

He heals the brokenhearted and binds up their wounds.

Psalms 147:3

In overcoming fear of the unknown, God was asking me to have more faith in Him. I thought this would be easier for me, but there were areas in my life that needed to be restored. The thick walls I had built up concerning my relationship with my dad, and even my in-laws, had to come down, and I needed to forgive. How was I going to help all these young people if I was damaged myself? How could I ask someone else to forgive when I myself had not forgiven? How could I ask someone else to let go if I myself had not let go?

As I have been looking into the stages of healing God has for us, I see myself in most of them: broken heart, fearful heart, angry heart, hopeless heart, hard heart, and a numb or checked-out heart. God had work to do with me. My heart was hurt. Family, past relationships, and friends all contributed to my hurts. God loves us so much, and He wants to take those walls down, but we have to say yes and open the door for Him to do the work in us.

My dad was a Pierce County deputy. This was hard for a young girl growing up in the sixties. There was not a day I was not called a name or many names because my dad was a policeman. The feeling of rejection was huge here for a young girl who wanted to fit in. I was proud of my dad. When the other kids called me a pig's daughter (and other disgusting names), I would push up my nose and snort. I would not let them know they were hurting me.

Many times when my siblings and I were playing in the backyard, our neighbors, who'd had a few unhappy interactions with cops, decided to let us know what they thought of us and our dad. At eight or nine years old, I heard nasty names and words I'd never heard before, and it didn't feel good. I built up walls so I did not react to the hurt inside me, and I didn't let people know that they hurt me. This behavior only added to the many life experiences that began to build other big walls in my young life. The name calling ended when I was a young teen; however, the feelings of rejection and abandonment came in other forms as I got older.

Besides classmates and friends, family sometimes can be the hardest on us. Being the oldest has its good and bad issues. My parents expected me to be strong and independent, and they forgot I was just a child in need of their love. As a daughter, the love of a father is so important, and growing up, I yearned to have my dad's acceptance and love. Instead I felt rejection and disappointment, and those feelings stayed with me for a very long time. I built walls around my heart, I felt this was a way of keeping that hurt away; instead it just made the wall bigger, leaving a hole that desperately needed to be filled.

Then I married Steve and thought I was part of a family unit that could fill the gaping hole in my heart, but once again I was disappointed. Just as the relationship with my family was hard, my relationship with my in-laws was even harder. Marrying into a family can be good, and you can truly become a son or daughter, but instead of being a part of a family, I was an outsider.

My father-in-law was great and was a lot of things my dad was not, which I appreciated. I had a fear of my dad. He was strict, mainly because he saw so many youth that he arrested, who weren't doing good things, and he wanted to make sure we didn't turn out that way. He sometimes used his authoritative attitude with us; his look and voice alone were scary. That fear carried into the relationship I had, or didn't have, with my father-in-law and older male figures. I never allowed myself to get too close to them.

As I grew older, people I thought were like family were very hurtful, and grudges that were held for many years were repaid, even after the incident was long forgotten. They would do something to pierce your heart. One incident, when my sister-in-law was making a point of not letting me hold my newborn nephew at his baby shower but making sure everyone else did, was very hurtful to me. I sat with my daughter, who was six at the time, and watched my sister-in-law pass my newborn nephew to everyone, including my husband's ex-wife, but making sure I never got too close to him.

I kept my composure until I walked out the door. When I reached my car, the tears began to flow, and the sobs started. My poor daughter didn't know what to do. We called my husband, who wanted to confront his sister, but we both knew that would only give her the satisfaction that she did what she intended to do. This was something she kept for ten years, and it was all because of something I had done unintentionally. I found this all out months later in a phone call when she told me that what she did was payback for not asking my mother-in-law and her to hold my baby right after I got home from the hospital ten years before. That incident had been long forgotten by me, but not her. To protect myself, my walls would become thicker, like Stonehenge.

And then on top of all that, being a stepmother is really challenging. We had full custody of Steve's son, so I was a full-time mom, but I needed to remember that he already had a mom, and she didn't need to be replaced. I crossed a line with my stepson, and I hurt myself. I lowered my thick, massive walls, and loved the boy as my own, only to feel rejected once more by my stepson. This time the hurt was much deeper. I felt I gave so much but then found myself being reminded too many times by other family members, "You are not his mother. He doesn't care about you," and many other things that caused those walls to come back up.

While I was spending some alone time with God, He shared with me why I needed to share about my hurts and who hurt me. I didn't understand; then He said, "Because you felt rejection, unworthy, and not part of something you thought mattered. Family is supposed to be supportive and loving, but sometimes they are far from it. This is something the youth you deal with feel all the time." That broke my heart, but it is so true.

I felt much rejection in my young life by people I thought loved and cared for me, which is one thing I can truly relate with the homeless youth I see each week. Why do people who tell us that they care do things that hurt so deeply? And though we may never know that answer, in many ways, it's true that hurt people hurt people, and those hurting people have let things consume them. And most of the time, they do not look to God for help through those times. God showed me my dad's hurts, and as I grew older, the hurts turned into a wonderful gift of compassion for my dad and others.

May 16, 2013, was the day my hurting, thick walls came tumbling down. That was also the day of our women's retreat. I dreaded going, I didn't know very many of the women, and I knew that most of them had their friends they hung out with, but God always has a way of bringing you the right person to spend time with. Shelly was just like me, new to the group and a little uncertain, and we hit it off. We spent the two days together, laughing, sharing, and becoming friends. He knew who I needed to be with.

On Saturday, the woman leading the retreat asked us to write a love letter from God. She encouraged us to understand what God was saying to each of us. I had never done a letter like this before. As I rolled the pen between my fingers, I wondered if I would truly hear from God. What was He going to say to me? I prayed and asked Him to tell me how He felt about me. And He spoke these words very clearly to me:

> Sunshine, I love you; you are My gift. Your love for Me is pure and strong. Your heart is pure and full of love. Your worship is divine. You are My daughter, and I love you. Let

go of your pain. Let it go to me for I will replace it with much joy. Your heart is pure and full of love and giving. You are loved and have always been loved. You are My sunshine, and I will always love you. You are My precious one. Many more tears and much joy. Let go, let Me in, let go of all your pain that you have buried for so long. I will replace it with love and compassion. You are loved always. Pain, rejection, unloved, betrayal, unworthiness—you need to let them all go to Me. For you are worthy.

As I wrote down those words, I was bawling. I have never in my life cried as hard as I did that afternoon. My thoughts were, *Wow, God loves me and wants to take all my pain. How could He want that ugly pain I have kept inside and buried for so long? This is the Father I have been looking for—one who shows His love for me and tells me He loves me!* When I felt His presence, I felt His arms around me, giving those daddy hugs that I so longed for. He was healing me.

This was the beginning of a huge breakthrough for me. A jackhammer began to bust off pieces of my wall. I could feel the chunks of pain like bricks come away from my heart. I was about to scream out as the tears were falling down my face, so I covered my mouth so as not to scare the other ladies as they, too, were writing down the words God was giving them. My heavenly Father was healing my heart and giving me an acceptance and love like I have never known before. Being healed of so much hurt is almost like having surgery; you know you need it, but boy, it isn't fun having it done, and it hurts. That is how I felt. I needed this, but in letting God in, I was hurting. He wanted to take that away and replace it with so much peace, so much love. He was raining down on me big-time. This was an amazing experience and one that I was so thankful for because it was the start of my becoming who God needed me to be.

But this was just one time when God was breaking off large chunks of pain and hurt. I had a lot more chunks that needed to come off. I did not realize I had fifty years of hurts buried deep inside of me and was just hurting myself. I thought I had forgiven all of it and let go, but I realized I had not. God was saying it was time to let go because He has such love and concern for me.

When God heals us, it is like peeling an onion. There are different layers. He peels away all the layers, and even though I thought I had forgiven people, God would take me deeper. Additionally I was hurting my relationship with God. How could I go to Him with unforgiveness in my heart? I needed to be free so I could do my best with what He called me to do. Genesis 16:13 speaks of Hagar, who was also hurting, yet God was close to her: "She gave this name to the Lord who spoke to her: 'You are the God who sees me,' for she said, 'I have now seen the One who sees me.'" God showed me that He saw me too! And He sees you too! I thought by having those walls I was a strong woman, but those walls made me weak. The walls consumed too much of me. By allowing God to tear down those walls, I became stronger—a free woman who could love and forgive.

After I got home from the retreat, later that night, we went to a fundraiser. A young woman shared her testimony. She had been abused in her younger years, then as a means to escape, she got into drugs and into bad relationships, and one ended in pregnancy. Thank God she found a home for unwed mothers and learned about the love of Jesus for her and her child. He life turned around because someone cared for and showed her what real love was all about.

After hearing her story, it was like God was saying, *Now you know why I need you to let go.* Some of the homeless youth carry a lot of hurt and have been badly damaged. I needed to be free and to let God in and start to do His mighty work inside me and inside the youth I would work with. I was to love these kids like he loves me. God wants me to love them unconditionally, and to have no judgment. To be there when they need someone the most. To give them hope when they feel they have none. And yes, to love them all; no child should be unloved.

God showed up big-time in my life during a time when I needed Him most. He showed me that even though I had been hurt, He could take that hurt away. He could free me, and He could change that unforgiveness into forgiveness and compassion. As I moved forward with the ministry, this healing showed me that I needed boundaries. I was a mother figure to the kids we were to serve, but I was not their mom. I could love them and care about them, just like God did. By saying yes to God, I allowed Him to come in, heal me, and begin to help me properly love the kids He wanted me to minister to.

Dear heavenly Father, I come to You brokenhearted and ask that You come in and mend my heart. Come in and show me the areas that need healing so that I can move forward with what You have for me. Thank You for loving me so much that You want me to be the person I was meant to be. In Jesus's name, amen.

CHAPTER 5

Trusting God in All Things

Cast all your anxiety on Him because He cares for you.

1 Peter 5:7

Four months into the M2M ministry, I was beginning to feel the need to rethink working at the bank. I fasted and prayed a lot. On June 2, 2013, I had my answer concerning my job. I went up during the church service for prayer one more time to confirm God was calling me into ministry full-time. This is what I received: "A tree starts small, but the roots are going deeper, and the tree is getting bigger."

God reminded me of how I trusted God to take care of me when I was a little girl. Now He was asking me to be like that little girl again and trust Him. He would take care of me when I quit my job at the bank. But before I decided to do anything, my husband had to be in complete agreement with me. On the way home from church, Steve and I spoke about what I was going to do, and my husband was in complete agreement. I went home and wrote my letter of resignation. I was excited and a little bit afraid. This was a huge leap of faith.

Steve and I were going to have to totally trust God with this. I was leaving total security, and now had to trust God to pay our bills. Steve's retirement wouldn't pay all the bills, so having complete faith that God would take care of us and all our needs was going to be a challenge. I gave my boss six weeks notice. When I handed him the letter, he did not believe me. He probably thought I would do the ministry when I had spare time, which was none if I continued working. I worked forty hours a week, and with the drive time one hour each way, my workdays were ten-hour days. With that schedule, there was no way I could fully do what I felt God was asking me to do.

Now that I had put in my work notice, it was time to get really serious about making Mother 2 Many a reality. Our son-in-law took on the job of getting our website up and running. As I looked at the website he created, I could not believe this was really happening. Our son-in-law and I have not always seen eye to eye, and this piece was a start of a wonderful healing and forgiveness. He had slowly worked himself into our family and become one of us. We could not imagine life without him. God was working miracles and healings in other areas as we began this journey.

Later in June, I went to church and could feel the presence of the Lord so strongly. I knew there was a message for me. Believe it or not, the service was on trust, a subject God was trying to teach me. I wanted to trust God but was finding it very hard to do. After the message, I felt I needed to go up for prayer and told Steve.

He said, "I know. I believe you will be going up there a lot, for you are going to need it." He did not realize that it would be the both of us going up there a lot as time went by. There was a specific woman, Debbie, that I needed to go to, but she was with someone, so I patiently waited. Another trait God was teaching me. So many things I needed to learn!

When I was able to get prayer, Debbie asked what I wanted prayer for. "God will tell you," I told her.

She was a little surprised, but as we started praying, she said, "I see a mother's heart. Is it broken?"

I said, "God has put us into ministry called Mother 2 Many." We were both in awe of God and what He was saying. Another confirmation of what He was calling me to do.

Now we have gotten into about six months of preparing and getting ready for what God wanted us to do. But we were still not ready to go out. One thing I learned is that the youth we would be dealing with need to be treated the right way. They already have a lot going on for them emotionally, so we must be careful, or we could make it much worse. I did not want to cause any further problems for them. I began to learn, one day at a time.

One lesson I learned was not to let anyone push you but instead wait on God's timing. I also learned that even though there are people who seem to have the same heart, they may not be as devoted as you are to the calling or task at hand. I had two of my team step away. A friend told me that would happen, but I didn't need to get discouraged. Sometimes that is really hard to do, not get discouraged. There were times I wanted to scream, *What is the matter with you, don't you know these kids need our help?* Yet in those times, I needed to remember God would bring the right people who were available and who had the same vision and motivation.

The first part of July, we went to church, and I received another word.

You're standing in a pond and there are many waves coming at you, but do not be discouraged. You need to stand firm and continue the journey. Do not dive into the water too soon, for it is not deep enough, and there is a possibility of hitting a rock. Wait until the water is deeper.

God wants me to wait and grow stronger. I need to be strong when I start this journey. There will be many obstacles, and I need to be fit to conquer them or I will fail. I cannot let it fail; I will not let it fail. God has told me that there are times you will hit a pothole in the road and you may get a flat tire, but will that stop you from still pushing forward? No, you get your tire fixed and you move on. There are just times when you need to hit the pothole to refocus and go the right direction. This was something I would need to remember later.

The youth we were going to help needed us, they needed us more than we may ever know. Life has changed for the youth of today, it is hard for them. So much peer pressure on each of them, and it starts young. God's work on me was going to help the youth we served. I could go forward knowing I was OK, and I know by loving them just like Jesus, they too can become overcomers.

God was preparing us in moving forward in the ministry, but most importantly, He was healing my heart and making me stronger. God was giving me His heart, just like David—a heart that was humble, reverent, respectful, trusting, loving, devoted, recognizing, faithful, obedient, and repentant. It started with saying yes to God and opening my heart for Him to heal me. I wasn't perfect. I had a past, which has made me who I am today. I want to be like David, a woman after God's own heart.

> *Dear heavenly Father,* I come to You with an open heart. I want to trust You in all things. I want to have Your heart, Lord, and want to love like You love. Teach me, Lord, to do what You want me to do. In Jesus's name, amen.

CHAPTER 6

Let's Get the Ball Rolling

Surely God is my salvation; I will trust and not be afraid. The Lord, the Lord, is my strength and my song; he has become my salvation.

Isaiah 12:2

On July 16, 2013, I went to work for the last time. My journey as a mother to many was beginning. I felt at peace, knowing I was doing the right thing. I was excited to start working for my heavenly Father.

I said my goodbyes, and even though I was sad to leave my wonderful coworkers, I was looking forward to an exciting future with Mother 2 Many. It is amazing that when you step out and share with a few friends what you are doing, then doors begin to open. After sharing with a friend about M2M, she suggested I meet with Julie. She oversaw the Buckley Family Center and had worked with other organizations that helped those in need. Since we were still not totally sure of where God wanted us, we talked to anyone that dealt with the homeless and youth. Julie was in her forties, with blond hair, and a smile that made you feel totally welcome. She was a wonderful encouragement and gave us a name of a few more people to go talk to, and then they did the same. Our first meetings were mainly to learn, understand, and to get help with getting started. Julie was the best person to talk to, and she has remained a dear friend.

Now that I was done working at the bank, we were able to finish my office. I needed to make M2M official. Steve made shelves for the office, and they were like bookshelves but housed toiletry items. My son Josh made a prayer bench, which has been the perfect spot in my office. It is my place to go first thing in the morning to talk to my Father, and for Him to talk to me. It is my time to be silent, which is extremely hard for me to do. My brain does not stop working; it goes in every direction.

At my prayer bench one day, burdened for the many teens Steve and I would reach out to, my mind was thinking about all sorts of things. I felt God telling me that love was a key word. No hate or judgment needs to be shown to these young people, only God's love. In this ministry we need people who trust and believe in what God can do, who will take a leap of faith and not be afraid to be warriors for Christ, who are willing to stand firm and be bold. With God for us, who can be against us? God is so good; this was exactly what He wanted to really put into our hearts. All this prepared us for what God really was calling us to do.

These are the specific truths God put on my heart:

- Be strong in all things.
- Listen when your heart says no.
- Keep on the path that God has set you on; do not waiver.
- Look to Him and stand firm.
- Remember who you are.
- The Lion of Judah is leading you and protecting you.
- Do not be afraid, for He is with you always.
- Love those kids no matter what, for they are mine.
- Look past all their past sins.

Next was making sure M2M was set up as a nonprofit organization. That took a lot of work and at times felt as if Mother 2 Many would never get off the ground. But we did and were recognized as a nonprofit. Soon it became apparent that I needed someone to do our bookkeeping, but we did not have the money to spend on a bookkeeper. A woman at church gave me the name of someone who did taxes. I met with her and as we began talking, I was surprised how much she charged—and even more surprised that she wouldn't charge us for the year or even the next year. What a godsend! Once again God was looking out for us.

After getting the office set up and a bookkeeper in place, we began meeting with more people who had been referred to us through Julie and others who had the heart for the youth experiencing homelessness. This was the beginning of doing what God told us to do.

Our pastor shared "If you say you can help, then you must be able to help." This was one of the things that God kept impressing upon my heart, if you say you are going to do something, do it. Always follow through. We were going to meet as many people as possible. We needed to start getting toiletry items, hats, and gloves to give out to those in need. I was excited because I knew the more I learned, it would get me that much closer to working with the youth.

As Steve and I traveled meeting with organizations, people, and centers, I discovered that the biggest need was a home for youth. As we talked to more people, and heard what they felt was most needed, my busy mind started drifting from God's plan. The skate park started to fade away, and my focus started to go toward a home for homeless youth

In my time of prayer and trying to focus on what God wanted us to do, God gave me some verses:

But the wisdom from above is first of all pure. It is also peace loving, gentle at all times, and willing to yield to others. It is full of mercy and good deeds. It shows no favoritism and is always sincere. And those who are peacemakers will plant seeds of peace and reap a harvest of righteousness. (James 3:17–18 NLT)

As we shared with a few people what we felt God wanted us to do, we had a meeting at our home. We had about five people come, all strong people of faith from different walks of life. A young man about twenty-five came to the meeting. I had seen him at church and loved how he interacted with the youth and how on fire he was for the Lord, and he was very happy when I asked if he would like to join us for our first meeting. His name was Brad. As we all sat and just talked, I could see him drawing something, and then he gave me a picture. He said, "Here are you, and under you are us; you are to teach us, and we will teach others." (I learned that the Lord confirmed this later.)

Brad drew me a picture and a diagram of what he was trying to have me see, and then wrote down this Scripture: "'For my thoughts are not your thoughts, neither are your ways my ways,' declares the Lord. 'As the heavens are higher than the earth, so are my ways higher than your ways and my thoughts than your thoughts'" (Isaiah 55:8–9). This has stuck with me ever since he gave it to me.

From July to December 2013, Steve and I had met a lot of people. We traveled over three thousand miles. And God provided for us. Even when Steve went back to work, God brought me someone who could attend meetings with me. At one time she had been an addict and homeless, and I learned a great deal from her.

As 2013 ended, and we looked forward to a new year, I saw it as a year of new beginnings and acceleration. God was not working slowly, but He was working faster. I hoped 2014 would bring new ideas and new direction that God had for us.

It had been six months since I quit my job, and it was the start of a new year. January 2014 started off slow, but that was OK, for we had been busy, and we didn't need to burn ourselves out. I signed up to go with our Women of the Word Bible study to visit the girls at Teen Challenge. How cool, since the first book I read, *The Cross and the Switchblade*, was about the founding of Teen Challenge. It is amazing how God works and brings things around to a full circle. This outreach had become very dear to me, and I asked to go with the ladies every time they went.

It was wonderful to meet so many young women that had decided to get off addiction and make huge changes in their lives. We met in the living room of a big house that houses up to twenty girls. The setting was one of family; everyone was welcome, and all the girls there were very attentive to hearing what we had to share. We were all sitting together in a large circle, so everyone could be seen.

When we met, someone shared with them a testimony or encouraging message. We then got to pray with the ladies, and each time God highlighted certain ladies that I got to speak life into. To see them smile and cry tears of joy was so amazing. I usually always cried with them, and eagerly listened to their stories of what God had done in their lives. God let us be a ray of sunshine for these girls.

I later got to speak to the women here at this home and shared my story of my past. This was not easy; I was also sharing my story in front of ladies I went to church with. But to my surprise, no one looked at me as if I were anyone different from the person they first met at church. They, too, had a story, and most of us had a similar road. It was wonderful to share with these ladies my story, and to my amazement, many also felt the pain of rejection, unworthiness, and being unloved. It was a way of connecting to these ladies, and it was part of my healing too.

On February 26, I met with two different organizations. One was from the school district, and the other was a pastor from a Methodist church.

The two women from the school district were amazing. They both had a heart for the homeless and were women of faith, so a bonus. One of them told me that she could feel the spirit just pouring out of me. Just amazing since my prayer that morning was to have the love of Jesus come out of my pores. I wanted to shine with God's love, and I did! I believe that I will have a growing friendship with these two women. We all can help each other in this walk to help the young that need so much help and direction. But, most of all, just love.

Then I met with Pastor Pam from the Methodist church. I had not met her before but through a contact, we got to talk. Pastor Pam has been in this community for a long time and has a very good reputation for helping youth. She was very eager to hear what I had to say. We met at her office at the church, and she shared with me what they had been doing with the community, and then she showed me her church building. It is a beautiful old church with stained glass window, dark wood trim and staircases, and large rooms to have a meal or study.

I shared what I wanted to do, not knowing what would be said later. She then shared what they were doing with youth in the Sumner area, which is what I was told, but then she started talking about having a drop-in center at their church. A drop-in center is usually in a building with an open area that youth can go to. It is always supervised with usually two to three adults. They will have snack items for the youth to eat, games for them to play, and even someone that can help them with homework if needed. It is a safe place for youth to go, to help keep them out of trouble. Since we had detoured from the skate park idea, the youth center idea had piqued my interest for a bit. As I was listening, I was thinking, *Am I hearing her right?* This was not in concrete, but she was going to talk to some people in her church, and we would pray about this. We would talk again soon. When I got to my car I said, "Lord, You just surprised me, and You are so amazing."

The six months after quitting my job had been eventful. I had worked full-time on the ministry and then had taken that step to find out as much as I could about homelessness. All that is part of homelessness—sex trafficking, addiction, mental illness. In some cases, parents kick their kids out of the house for a new boyfriend, or the youth does not feel safe at home and feel they have no other option but to run away; they then live at friends' homes, which is called couch surfing, or the worse part, live on the streets. This truly breaks my heart, and at times could be overwhelming for someone who knew nothing about the world of homelessness. God was teaching me so much, and I knew I needed to know these things to help me understand their world, something I knew nothing about.

All these things worked together and were all areas that I had known nothing or little about. I met people from organizations in all those areas. God was definitely having me learn, and now I saw why my heart needed to change and why I needed to heal. I could not go out and help if I were all messed up. He was showing me by

LET'S GET THE BALL ROLLING

meeting with young women who were getting out of addiction, that they were little girls at one time too, with dreams and visions for their futures. Life problems got in the way, but they were still that little girl, crying for help.

This also applied to teen boys. Even though it was easier for me to relate to girls, God was teaching me that I would be dealing more with boys than girls. Boys were easier to work with; girls can shut themselves off just like I did; yet they both had similar hurts and struggles. I needed to remember that as I continued learning and working with various groups of people on this journey. Later as we began working with the youth, we would see eighty boys to twenty girls, a big difference.

God is so good. He is right there with me. He guides me and teaches me. There were times I felt all alone in this journey, but then God would bring someone to me who assured me I wasn't. He brought me a dear friend, Judy, whom I attend church with. She was a bit older than me but the sweetest lady. She had been my Bible study leader a few times, and one day she and I had lunch at Applebee's. The hostess sat us at a nice corner booth by the window, and no one was around us. We ordered our food, and as we waited she told me this. "As I was driving, God showed me a lone tree on the hill, and that was you. But as I drove the tree began to be surrounded by other trees, showing you that you were not alone, that He was bringing others to help you." My eyes filled with tears as I heard those words, God hadn't left me alone, He was right there, and He was preparing others to come alongside us. I'm not alone in this.

With all the donations we have gotten, it has been wonderful to take our donations and give them to places that hand out the toiletry items and socks. We have been blessed with so much, and it is wonderful to be able to help so many others with what we have. Also, when we give out, God brings in a ton more, so that is great to see also. Isaiah 58:10–11 reminded me that "If you spend yourselves in behalf of the hungry and satisfy the needs of the oppressed, then your light will rise in the darkness. And your night will become like the noonday." I love the sun; I love the rays that the sun puts out there, and as I start to see things fall into place, I see the sun/Son. Our office has a large sun in it, our brochures have a sun on them, and I know we will have more large bright suns on all that Mother 2 Many has. A ray of hope, a ray of sunshine in this very dark world these youth live in. God's sunshine!

Dear heavenly Father, thank You for choosing me to do Your will. You have set me apart because You have a plan for me. Help me to see that plan. Help me to learn from those You send my way to help. Thank You, Father, for what You have for me. In Jesus's name, amen.

Chili or Chile?

*For I know the plans I have for you, declares the Lord, plans
for welfare and not for evil, to give you a future and a hope.*

Jeremiah 29:11 ESV

The summer of 2013, our pastor started talking about a mission
trip to Iquique, Chile, to go in the spring of the next year. Since
we were just getting started with Mother 2 Many and starting
to learn more about what God wanted, I just let it go to dead ears.
The next week once again we were at church, and once again pastor
shared about going to Chile. Something hit me this time: *Could this
be another way of learning about serving and helping those in need?*

Steve and I had never thought about going to another country;
we were totally focused on M2M. Something was tugging at me to
check into this further. This was truly exciting since I never even
dreamed of doing a mission trip, and now I felt God was pulling me
in that direction—new, learning, and just jump-out-of-the-car-and-
dance exciting. At church one Sunday Gary, the head of missions,
once again talked about going to Chile.

I mentioned my desire to Steve on the way home. "Hey, what do
you think about Chile?"

He then replied with a questioning look on his face. "You can
make any chili you like."

Steve always has a way of making me laugh, and this was no
exception. I chuckled at his humor, realizing how he interpreted the

word. Easy to do for a guy. Then with a smile on my face I said, "Not chili. The mission trip to Chile." I was excited to find out that he, too, had been thinking of going to Chile.

I decided to do a seven day fast, always a great way to really hear from God on things you are not sure about. When I fast I also have dreams, and dreams have meaning. All this was very new to me; when I had dreams before, they were always stupid dreams I would always forget by morning. Now I was seeing very vivid dreams with colors and words I could hear and understand. It was truly amazing. Here is one of my dreams:

> I was at the bus or train station, and there was a young girl there. I asked her if she had a place to go, and she said no, so I asked if she would like to come to my house. She said yes. Upon arriving, the house was huge. Inside there was another young girl hanging from a basketball hoop, getting ready to jump to the floor. The basketball hoop was three stories high and this house had at least five stories to it; it was a really big house. My heart leaped into my throat. I yelled to her, "No! You cannot jump! We must set an example for the world outside because this home is one of a kind."

I had the dream interpreted by a friend who interprets dreams and what was said excited me. It gave me hope and let me know that we were going in the right direction, even when it felt like we were not. Also, God revealed much more to me much later. I have found that in everything we have done, and things He has shown me from the start that it isn't always revealed right away. This dream took about two to three years until He really told me all that it meant. Here is what He told me: M2M was the home, us the people, and we needed to make sure that we did everything right. M2M skate park outreach was one of a kind, and people were watching us. We needed to be fun, childlike, loving those kids right where they were at. This was exciting, something new. I would have a few more dreams later, but this particular one hit home the most.

I was excited to hear what else God wanted for us, and after my fast, I felt we were to move forward. We were ready for the mission trip. We sent in our applications, and they were accepted. Besides having faith in raising money to go to Chile, Steve and I needed to learn some of the language, and Steve got a book on Chile so we could understand their culture. It was important to understand the people and where we were going. God came through with the finances to go, and it came in the very last day, once again teaching us to have total faith in Him.

The day had come and it was time to pack and go to the airport to start our new journey as missionaries to another country. This was very exciting, something so new, and we were once again doing something we knew nothing about. Again faith was instrumental in teaching us not to fear the unknown. Steve and I were doing something we never dreamed of doing. And yet by embarking on this mission trip, we were stepping out on faith, adding to our tool bag life lessons and experiences that would help us as we continued building the foundation of our ministry. We were totally in unknown territory, once again trusting God to walk before us and direct us.

When we arrived at the airport, we learned the first lesson on trusting God into the unknown. Our flight was delayed. We got to Georgia, but late, so we missed our connecting flight to Chile. We had to stay in Georgia overnight, and we arrived in Chile twenty-four hours later than planned. That was a lesson in great patience. Without knowing the language, there were language barriers, and thank goodness, most people at the airport spoke a bit of English.

We finally arrive in Iquique, Chile. It is a beautiful place. Right in front of the city is the ocean, and behind it is the desert. You have areas that are very nice for the tourists, but once you drive outside of those areas, it is very poor, and the buildings and houses show that. They are rundown with broken windows, plaster coming off the houses, and garbage in their yards—very depressing. We settled into our place, which was a small apartment with four bedrooms, clean but not a Hilton. We rested for the day, met the pastor we would be helping, and we ate a wonderful meal and got some much needed sleep.

So many things could have stopped us from being excited for what we were about to do in Chile, but even with the delays God was working with us and our team. Most of the people welcomed us, and we loved meeting so many different people. The next day we headed up to Putre, a town that is eleven thousand feet above sea level. Most of the team experienced high-altitude sickness, even though we were taking pills to help us. They were cocaine candy. They reminded me of cough drops, but they were green, and they were not addictive, but they were supposed to open up your vessels to help you breathe better. I think my migraine medicine helped better and used that to help with the headache and was able to share with another team member who got a real bad headache. Not a fun experience. We did everything very slowly; that way we didn't overexert ourselves and use up oxygen we were having a hard time getting. We were in Putre for four days, and we hoped to adapt, but that didn't happen.

We had arrived in Putre later in the day and got to settle in. Even a village that has dirt roads and maybe one restaurant has a hotel. This was really nice. Steve and I had our own room and a shower, small rooms but very clean. That night as we prepared for the next day's journey, we sat outside of the hotel, and since there were no city lights, the sky was lit up with stars, millions of stars, and there were shooting stars. It was like the sky was full of shining diamonds, something I had never seen before. What a true blessing to see the beautiful masterpieces that God has made. Something I will never forget.

The third day in, our team was able to go and minister to some of the children in little villages. The people live in little shacks made out of rocks and mud, and they have mud with tree branches for their roofs. Most do not have power. The shacks have dirt floors, but a regular door, and they have a fire pit for heat. We saw a lady out washing her clothes, and she just had a bucket and a board to wash her clothes with. The people were very friendly, mainly because they knew one of our hosts, Renee, who was the pastor in Putre. What a joy it was to give out lollipops and homemade knitted hats to the children. The villagers were very poor, so a lot of the items they had were secondhand items, worn and even had holes in them. Since they were so high up, this clothing was truly needed to keep warm. The kids swarmed the vans that we were in and were jumping up and down to make sure they got their lollipop. Candy is something we can get easy in the States, but here it was a treasure.

One thing we found out was that in the little villages they practiced witchcraft. It was one of their main religions, and because of that, some did not like us being there. Renee was trying to change that, but it was a slow process. As we drove up to each village, people would come out and talk a bit; some would go back into their houses. Since I was not feeling the best from the high altitude, I stayed in the van, which was disappointing, but I watched from the window and saw how our team was.

We came to a ranch, and they had alpacas, and it was so cool to see about thirty of them. The farmer seemed very nice, and eager to show off what he had. He had a stone barrier keeping his alpacas in place. The workers looked like cowboys with their straw hats, jeans, flannel shirts, and boots. Their hands were worn from working hard, and their faces were weathered from the sun and, in the winter months, cold. Going up to the villages, we hit sixteen thousand feet, but the country was beautiful.

There were not a lot of trees, but beautiful rolling hills, and the mountain gave Mt. Rainier some competition. Then it was time to head back to Putre before it got dark. We had dinner with Renee and his family. His home was very small; a handmade table was used to sit at with worn-out chairs that did not match. The kitchen had a small heating element to cook food, and water had to be brought in to wash dishes.

After dinner everything was moved, a few benches were put into place on the dirt floor, and this was where they had church. About ten people showed up—having people come from another country to share was a real treat for them. These people were learning about Jesus and were all newer believers. They were all hungry to hear what we had to say, and even though we had to have Aaron interpret for us, it was a wonderful time of sharing and praying with these wonderful people of Putre. When I shared, I shared about being a mother to many and how God was teaching me that it didn't matter the age, but to love all that came to us. After I was done and we had a time to pray, a lady who was small and petite came to me in tears, wanting prayer. She had a child she had not spoken to in a long time, and my message touched her heart. As I prayed with her, using our interpreter, the lady and I were both crying and praying for God's goodness and restoration of her relationship with her child. At the end of the prayer we hugged. God's love was working here.

The night after speaking to Renee's members, I had a visitor. I was asleep. The room was pitch-black; you couldn't see your fingers in front of your face; but suddenly, I could see very clearly in my mind that there was a little old lady in the corner of the room. It was like she was sitting in the corner, looking down, with a scarf on her head and a long ruffled dress and long, gray, messed up hair. I could tell she was old by her hands, which she was rubbing together; they were wrinkly and worn for hard work and age. She reminded me of a witch doctor, and she was mumbling something that I could not hear.

I was really frightened, and I couldn't get to the light switch fast enough. It was on Steve's side of the bed, so I had to crawl over him, and of course, this woke him up, yet he was still somewhat asleep and didn't understand. Once I got the light on, she was gone. It was midnight when I looked at the clock by the side of the bed, and we had to get up in four hours. It was going to be a very long night, but finally sleep came upon me, and we were up early in the morning to head back down the mountain and have a weekend of peace.

The weekend started off nicely. We did a family fair night and got to pray with families and got to really spend some time with the people of Iquique. It was nice to be able to get to interact with the people, and here it didn't matter that we couldn't speak their language or that we were from a different country. Everyone was here to have fun, to eat, to listen to the music, and just enjoy life. This was a great ending to eight days of travel, ministering, and encouraging those around us.

As we left the fair, we had dogs come alongside us, and they were leading us. There is a large population of dogs, and they can really be a problem, since they have no homes and are always looking for food. But this was different. As we were walking it was like they were protecting us, and it was more obvious when a man came walking toward us saying something. The dogs started to growl and bark at him. He quickly walked away, and the dogs walked us to our cars and then dispersed. This showed me that God will use anything to protect you, and the dogs were our protectors that day.

This trip taught us both a lot. God taught us to have faith, He brought in the means to pay for our trip, and He was with us through all the craziness that we went through. He taught me that, even though there was a language barrier between us and one of our hosts that could be comical at times. Renee would try to share something with us about his family, and our interpreter was there; we would use signs or try to find something in the room that would help us communicate. Or the one time we went shopping, and the lady at the counter got mad at me because I didn't know their language. She was yelling at me so loud the interrupter had to come over to calm her down. This was a bit unsettling, and I really didn't want to deal with this type of treatment, but to my surprise, other store owners were very nice and spoke some English. In this He showed me He could still work through us, the way we act or look says a lot to people. As time went on with our ministry, this really helped.

God gave us a love for these people. We did not know them, but they were God's children, and we are so extremely glad that we were able to go down and help them. I am even friends with a few people we met on Facebook. Also, stepping out was the biggest learning tool, not speaking the language was the biggest obstacle, but everything worked out. Going to Chile taught us we could do whatever God asked us to do and that we always needed to remember, *Fear not, for I am with you!*

After coming home, I was sick for the next two weeks. My body needed to rest. Mentally and physically, I was drained. I spent time in my Word and in prayer. I took a lot of naps. This was very new to me; I had never been so worn out for so long. But once I felt better, it still seemed as if a blanket was still smothering me. I felt like a heavy weight had attached itself to me. I was feeling better from the trip, but this was something deeper. It was like something had attached itself to me, and it was driving me crazy.

It was time for some serious praying, and I called some friends to come over so we could pray this through. Tina, Sue, and one other lady came to pray with me. I'm not good at asking for help, but this time I knew I could not do this on my own. I needed some strong prayer warriors to come alongside me and help me. After about an hour of praying and seeking God, I could feel the blanket lift. I was free from whatever had been holding me back. There are times when you need help, and this time God said, *Hey, you can't do this on your own*, and He brought amazing women to come alongside me.

Two days later the pastor said, "Your feet are in the Jordan. Be patient."

As I mulled the pastor's words and his sermon illustration, I knew these words were for me, and I wanted to listen. After the mission trip I wanted to go headfirst into whatever God had for us. I felt I had learned enough, but there was much more to learn, and being patient was one of the lessons. If I ran too fast into something, I could move in my timing and not God's. God was moving, and I just needed to make sure that my steps were His steps. I had a lot to think about and pray about before I did anything more with M2M.

During my time of rest, I had time to think about what I had learned on our mission trip, and also asked God what was next. I knew that now that I had been out doing missions, I was ready to do some more, but I knew it would not be in another country but right here at home. I felt God wanted me to start right where I lived, that my gifting was working with those in need, and caring for those people would be something I could really do. I learned that when we were down in Chile. I also learned that even though I didn't think I could work with youth, I could. Now it was time to really pray about where God wanted us to go.

I called some of my friends who were already walking alongside us in what God was asking us to do and asked if they wanted to go to Tacoma to feed the homeless. I was excited when they all said yes. Ten of us got together at our home and assembled Blessing Bags from all the items we had gathered from friends and places that had set up donation boxes at their workplaces. In each of the bags, we put gloves, hats, hand warmers, and nonperishable food items. We decided to bring a thermos of hot water for hot chocolate that we made up as we gave cups to any homeless that we came in contact with. This would be something nice to help to get them warm. If they had been spending their time outside, we also had blankets that had been donated to hand out.

This outreach took us downtown Tacoma. We walked about three miles around town, and we found a lot of people—young, old, women, men, and teens—who were experiencing homelessness. As I stood there in my nice warm coat, nice gloves that kept my hands warm, and a nice, knitted hat, I started to look at the people I saw in different areas on the street. One sat next to a building with a sleeping bag wrapped around them that had been well used and had dirt all over it. Someone cuddled with just a face showing in a corner next to a building with a pile of blankets that were worn and dirty and some just stood on the street smoking a cigarette, trying to stay warm, but moving in place or talking to another person close by—or even to themselves.

God started to show me what He saw: people who had been broken down; people with addictions, for reasons unknown of a life they had lived; someone's child; and most importantly, His children. My heart started to break for these people who seemed to feel all alone and forgotten. This was something I could do, because He asked me to, and I knew that He would help me along the way. I knew that we were not alone in doing this. He had brought others who had a love for the homeless. Even though I knew God wanted us to work with youth, I knew this was something we would do just for a season or two, but it was another way of God teaching us about homeless of all ages.

As we walked and looked for the homeless, we found that they would mainly be by a bus route, under bridges, in an alley, places away from people, unless they had gotten enough money by begging to buy some food. God was giving me eyes like an eagle; I could spot them. They usually always had a backpack, dirty clothes, messed up hair, sometimes a cart with all their belongings, or even a suitcase with wheels, following close behind. Some even had a dog for companionship. We would go up to them cautiously and ask if they would like something to eat, a blanket, and hot chocolate. We were never turned down.

From the start of the Tacoma ministry, we always offered to pray with each person we stopped to visit with. Some said yes, some said no, and we respected their wishes.

When praying for the homeless, there are times that can totally catch you off guard. As we were all walking, we spotted a young man, maybe in his twenties, a nice-looking man with brown hair, and a nice smile. He was sitting on the sidewalk with a blanket around him, so we knew most likely he was homeless. As we approached him, we asked if he wanted something to eat. He said yes and we also had a homemade scarf and gave that to him. When we asked him if we could pray for him, he was fine. But then he became someone else.

He took on an authoritative personality as if he was an undercover cop. I thought, *Oh my gosh, he's a cop.* Then he started yelling at us, asking us what we were doing feeding the homeless, that it was against the law, and we were in so much trouble. He used every curse word you could think of and kept saying he was a cop and he was going to arrest us. It scared me to death because I had never had this happen to me, and neither did my team.

We all stood there, looking at each other and at him as he continued to scream at us. It finally dawned on us; this man had a spirit that had attached itself to him that knew how to push our buttons. Believe me, he was very convincing, but when we all realized what was going on, we just said, "OK, you have a blessed day."

As we started to walk away, I looked at him, and he said in a very different voice, "You know he will never wear that scarf." If I could have, I probably would have run down the street faster than Flash Gordon, but I didn't want it to know it got to me. A very scary moment, but again, another teaching moment that helped in future situations.

This outreach lasted four years and was a time of learning once again. God was changing all our hearts when it came to adult homelessness. We would always stop for coffee halfway through our walk and just talk about the people we had met. I would hear from the other team members of how they once looked at a homeless person as a bum, some were afraid of them, and some would just ignore them. But by going into Tacoma, talking with so many nice homeless people, they realized they were just like you and me, but something had happened in their lives. Some would share what that was, and some would not. Homelessness is a very sad and lonely life.

Their stories broke my heart. People losing jobs, loss of family, drug and alcohol addictions—hurting people who felt they had no hope. Dealing with the spirit of the old lady in Chile helped me deal with the unknown of the street people.

There was an old lady, she was about sixty-five or older (hard to tell sometimes because of the hardship of living on the streets), and it was raining. Washington rain is the worst; you have the soft rain that soaks you no matter what you have on, and this was one of those days. Her dog was in a stroller all covered with blankets, and she had a thin coat on to keep warm and dry. Her dog was her life and more important than herself. Her frail hands were cold, and thank goodness we had a few things to help her, a blanket, gloves, hat, and some food. Something she really needed.

Teens who had been kicked out of their homes because of a new boyfriend had been dropped off on the streets to fend for themselves. Some had dealt with things that no one should ever have to deal with.

There were times people would manifest into something totally crazy. It always seemed to happen when we would ask if we could pray with them. They would say yes, but once we laid hands on them and started to pray, yelling would start, and a totally different person was in front of us. This is very unsettling, and not my favorite part of going into Tacoma, but something that only happened four or five times.

There is a park in the middle of Tacoma, and as we were walking by, we could see someone was living there. There were blankets made to be a covering with grocery carts all around, it looked like a large tent that a kid would have made in their backyard. As we passed by, God showed me what was living there; it was a person who was possessed big-time. He showed me a picture of Gollum from *Lord of the Rings* in my head. When I looked over closer, there was a person—I could not tell what sex—and they had long greasy hair, somewhat hunched over, with dirty clothes. It was trying to avoid us, and we did not go near. We were not trained to deal with that. My first responsibility was to keep my team safe, and that person was not safe. My spirit told me so. I have learned to listen to those warning bells, and my bells were ringing big-time.

Then there would be a few who would just come up to us and yell. We would just keep walking. That is the time to take authority, and we would say "Be quiet in the name of Jesus," and then silence, and they would walk away. We are all human, and there have been times I just want to run and get the heck out of there, but God reminds me that I am safe; no harm will come to us.

Thank goodness not all homeless are that way. Some are very nice and just want to sit and talk. We will do that at times and listen to their stories of maybe losing their job and losing everything after that. When they share these stories, you really must dig deep down and make sure you do not get too wrapped up with their stories, because sometimes it is just that, a story.

We were excited to finally step out and work with people experiencing homelessness and moving in the direction we felt God was leading us. After going once we decided to take a team out once a month and go into Tacoma. We would sometimes see people that we saw the month before, but most of the time it was new people. Seeing people on the street, they usually are not happy, but when we would come up to them, and ask if they wanted a lunch, a hat, scarf, and gloves, they would give you a nice smile, and were always so appreciative. Some would go on to tell us they were out looking for a job, or they weren't planning to be homeless long but just needed to get on the right track. Stories were heard a lot, but they always thanked us, and some would let us pray and some would say no. We were OK either way.

This outreach ministry became a training field for me to see that the people on the streets were human and needed to be treated in human ways. Loving the unlovable is what God was truly teaching me. I never thought I was a snobby person, but when I would see a homeless person before, I would just see a bum, a dirty person that needs to get a job. I thought that for years. Once I started to go out to the streets and to sit and talk with them, sometimes cry with them, my heart started to change. These were people. Yeah, they weren't living the way I would, but what right did I have to judge them; I didn't really know what brought them to where they were at that moment. All I could truly see was a broken person who once was a child with dreams and hopes for their futures, and now they had nothing.

God truly took my mind and had me rethink how I was to these people. I needed to love like Christ loved, I needed to not judge. I needed to be the person God was asking me to be and to truly love my neighbor as myself. On one of our trips, there was a dad who had three little kids with him. He was waiting for someone to pick them up. I could tell he did not have much, and the kids were poorly dressed for a cold day. Thank goodness we had gloves and scarves to hand out to them, and the little one, who was about a year or so, had a runny nose, so I picked him up and cleaned him up.

Our youth pastor looked over at me and told the group, "She's got this, she is doing what Jesus would do." This made me cry. I was doing what came naturally, helping this little one, and showing Jesus in what I was doing. God makes everyone a somebody, and no one is a nobody to God!

> *Dear heavenly Father,* I come to You and ask that You give me strength when I am going into the unknown. Even in my feelings of uncertainty and practice of faith, I remember You are with me always. When a door opens, I know You opened it. Let me go forward knowing You are right there beside me. I am not alone. In Jesus's name, amen.

CHAPTER 8

God Is Never Outdone

But Jesus looked at them and said, "With man this is impossible, but with God all things are possible."

Matt 19:26 ESV

During the first year of our Tacoma outreach, I learned that youth are hard to find out on the street. They are there, but they try to keep hidden, or they want to blend in. They couch surf and will stay at different friends' homes, live in their cars, or live in tents far from seeing eyes.

As we continued to move forward, I received confirmation after confirmation about the direction we were headed, and I was really excited. Before we went to Chile I had a dream where I met a young girl at a bus station and brought her back to our home that was very large and had a lot of kids there. So I thought maybe God wanted us to look for a home to house youth, and since I had received so many words about youth and being a mother to many, I thought this was the direction we were meant to go.

We received the Scripture from a friend, Deuteronomy 11:8–15, which talks about crossing the Jordan and climbing the mountain. About a land that is not like Egypt but a land that God loves. My feet are no longer in the Jordan; we are moving forward. I'm feeling very excited and confident that I'm doing what God has called us to do.

I love Christmas and, as a child, waiting for the day to open presents sometimes was unbearable. One time I sneaked upstairs to see what my parents got me. Christmas was ruined. I should have waited because then I could have enjoyed the joyful feeling of my parents buying me exactly what I asked for. Even though I was happy, the feeling was not the same. God was telling me that the best was yet to come, but I needed to take certain steps to get me where I was supposed to be, and timing is everything when doing what God has called us to do.

People in leadership were hearing about us. City officials, school district leaders, and church leaders were hearing the name Mother 2 Many. Most of these people have been working with youth in need for much longer than I, and I have gotten a few messages to meet with some of these people. This can be very scary and intimidating. As we moved forward with where we felt God was taking us, more people wanted to talk. To my excitement, our journey was starting, but crossing the Jordan and being on dry land, we needed to be a little slower in our walk because our next steps took us on a wrong journey, but a learning one.

In May 2014, I received a call from our pastor. He wanted to take us to a place he thought might be a place we could house youth for our ministry. I had shared with him I thought God might want us to have an actual home for homeless teens. We drove to the location. The building was an old Catholic church no longer used for services.

As we walked around, I saw our vision for Mother 2 Many come to life. I thought we could really make this into an amazing home for youth experiencing homeless, a safe place for them to live until they got their lives back on track or even reunited with their families. Was this where God was leading us? The tears began to flow as I could envision this place being a home for those who had no home. As we walked through this very large building, there was a rec center that could be used as a drop-in center. A dorm section, even though unfinished, could house forty-four youths. This was so wonderful, I wanted to scream with excitement, but that wouldn't have sat well with the neighbors. This was a wonderful building.

The house for youth was certainly a wonderful thing, but a questioning feeling nudged me. Was this God's dream, or was it mine? Did God want us to really have a home for homeless youth? There is so much that is involved in having a big home for youth, and I did not have a clue on running one. Food, twenty-four-hour monitoring, staff, clothing, schooling, and so on. This was something you really needed to have a college degree for; I have some college teaching, but not in all the areas that would be needed to run a home.

God was good, because He let me run with this for a bit, and there were reasons for that. I needed to wait to open that Christmas gift, but I looked before the big day. I needed to be patient and let the day come for the opening of God's gift. There is always good even though you may get a tad to the left or right. I met people I wouldn't have met, and I needed to know them later with M2M. Plus, I needed to learn to speak to Sumner city officials, and Sumner school district employees, and this helped me big-time because I had to meet with each one to move further with the house. You cannot just go buy a place and think I'm sticking a home for homeless youth right in a residential community without getting an OK; you have to go through all the proper channels, and there were a few channels to go through.

So now it was time to start meeting with city officials to get their approval of having a home in downtown Sumner. One important person I met was the assistant chief of police. I shared what we would like to do, have a home for homeless teens. He said he would like to help any way he could. I thought that was great. Having the police department on your side is always good. I have a bit of experience there with my dad, and it was always good to have a good relationship with the police.

Now that I had the support of the assistant chief of police, it was time to check on the zoning. Since I had forgotten about the skate park, I decided to go with the home for the youth and see what would happen. But God slowly began to close the doors.

I set up a meeting with the Sumner city planner. The planner was a very nice man and listened to me intently. I appreciated that, but what he told me left me a little discouraged. The area was not zoned for what we wanted to do, something I knew nothing about. I figured if you wanted to do something, you could do it, but there is red tape to everything. There was also money that you needed to have, over a thousand dollars to be exact, and it is nonrefundable. Something we did not have. He said to me, "You can meet with the city council and share what you want to do of having a home for homeless youth and win them over."

That would be the only way to change the zoning, to have the city council agree there was an issue with homeless youth and that the youth were from the Sumner area. The way he said it sounded like an easy task, but I found out it wasn't easy at all. The council looks at all issues: The neighborhood—will it be good for them, will it be bad for them? Will it bring in more problems for the area? And is there really that big of a problem with homeless youth in this area? Lots of questions that I didn't necessarily have answers for. I needed to walk a little slower after leaving the Jordan, but I was taking big steps into an area I really didn't know.

Also, when talking to the planner he told me before I really do anything further, Mother 2 Many needed to be a 501c3 before we could do what we wanted to do with this building. I had looked at the paperwork to become a 501c3, and that almost seemed impossible to me. But I knew if God wanted us to have this building, everything would work out. I sent a letter to the council on Sunday explaining what we wanted to do. The council met May 18. They had my number and told me my letter would be put on the agenda. It would be wonderful if they said yes, but if they said no, it meant God closed that door and would open another one. His timing and purpose would be perfect.

Finally, the city council called, asking me to share at their next meeting. I decided to fast for thirty-six hours in preparation. I have never done that before. I also needed to prepare talking points. I wrote down all the difficulties of homelessness, the amount of youth out there, and most importantly, the amount of youth in the Sumner area.

When I finished my points, I felt surprisingly good. I had a council member who thought what we wanted to do was great, and a few others that seemed on board. I just now had to wait to see what they all really thought, and the answer would come a few days later by email.

Once I got home, I feel a nudge to go outside and pray with Steve. We went outside and sat on the deck. I lit three candles, plus we had lights on the railing, displaying a beautiful scene. I looked up at the brightest star I have ever seen. It looked like a shiny diamond, and I smiled. All God's children are precious diamonds, each one unique. This was something I would always need to remember; so many youth do not feel this, they feel such rejection, so out of place, unwanted, and ugly. God wants them all to know how very loved they are. They are not a mistake, and they are all unique in His eyes. God was taking those blinders off my eyes. I needed to see that too.

Wednesday came, signaling the end of the thirty-six hour fast. God is good! I felt like I can do all things through Him, that I need to just trust Him, and He was so reassuring and comforting, in a time I truly needed it. Homelessness is not a fun subject, and everyone has their own ideas of what it is all about, and most think negatively about it. I wasn't sure how the council felt about homelessness. Was I going into a hornets' nest or into a caring bunch of people? I had no idea. I felt fasting was something I was going to do a few more times as M2M begins to evolve into what it is truly meant to be.

I walked three days a week with my friend. We had a good prayer time that encouraged me and energized me for the meeting that night to talk to some of the Sumner City Council. I was grateful for my friend's support. Even after praying with my friend, I felt the need to pray with more people who had supported me and had been there every step of the way on this M2M journey. I called my support group of ladies I went to church with and asked if they would pray with me.

A few hours later, after my time with my walking friend, I met with my friend Tina, who was a pastor of a church we sometimes attended, and a couple of other women at my home to help me feel at peace with the meeting later that night. At the end of prayer, Tina mentioned she could see God had put His hand on M2M, and no man can break what God had put His hand to. I was finding out and learning that when God tells you one thing or gives you a dream, it takes time for it to come to pass, God had given me M2M, and He wanted me to work with youth, but the full picture had not been shown. I was assuming God wanted one thing, and so I was going with it.

It was time for Steve and me to go down to the city hall building. It was Wednesday early evening, on a nice warm summer's day. As the council members arrived, I noticed each person. There were three council members of the planning committee, two women and one man, also city council members and also the community development director. One of the ladies asked me if I was part of the agenda. The director affirmed, and they put me at the top of the list instead of third. They had things to talk about that didn't involve me and felt it would be nice for me if I didn't have to sit there for forty-five minutes while they discussed other issues. This was a huge relief. I was very nervous, and having these people all staring at me as I shared my heart and would decide if the zoning changed and if we could have a home in the old church was a little disheartening. God was there, no doubt, because peace was starting to come over me, and I knew everything would be OK, no matter what they decided

I had ten minutes to share. I didn't think I would be able to cover all I needed to in the time they gave me. But I would sure try my best. The meeting was at city hall, so the setting was like a courtroom. They were on the other side of a fence-looking barrier. I had a podium to speak from. As the head council member brought the meeting to a start, he called my name, and then I was able to approach and share why I was there.

As I was talking, my friend Sarah from one of our church meetings showed up. The main entrance was to the right of me speaking, and when the door opened, it was by habit to look to see who it was. She walked in a little sheepishly because she got there late and ended up sitting right behind Steve. I thought she was here to talk too, so I continued my presentation. I felt the Holy Spirit was doing all the talking because in the ten minutes I was given, He brought up all the important information.

When I finished my talk, a few of the council members asked questions. As I talked, no one showed any reaction or emotions; they just sat there and listened intently. Once I was done speaking, one of the council members asked if what we wanted to do was even possible; two replied, yes it could be done. Then the discussion started about if there was even a need for this in Sumner, and one lady believed there was a need. At the end of me speaking, we were told we would go to the next level and speak to all the council, and that included speaking to the public. There was no conflict. The city council meeting went so smoothly, I was totally blown away.

One other thing I learned in all this is not to be intimidated by people in leadership, I talked to people I had never even dreamed of talking to, and God gave me confidence. He gave me the words to speak, which was the best part. When I spoke, people listened; they might not have agreed, but they listened.

As we got up to leave the room so the council could discuss other matters and our matter, Sarah followed Steve and me. Out in the hall, I turned and asked her why she'd come.

Her eyes brightened as she squeezed my hand. "Because I wanted to support you."

She had come just to support us, and had prayed while I spoke to the council members. God had my back, never leaving us in the dust. He brought us a young woman who heard what we were doing, and she listened to His calling.

While I waited to hear details for the next city council meeting, I sent thank you emails to everyone who attended. The one council member in charge emailed me back:

Yours is a noble venture. Scary, but noble!
One thing that I think would help a great deal is if you could present an example of where this is working. Where

a similar facility is in a residential neighborhood and folks see it in a positive light.

The default position for most people is, "Oh geez. We don't need a bunch of problem kids causing issues." That is the primary challenge. They will need to see real-life examples of where that is not the case. Thanks for the note. Best to you.

Reading this email, I felt anxiety, some fear, not knowing of other places that are doing the same thing I was wanting to do—fear, dread, and then a little bit of excitement. This was a challenge and another learning tool for me. I needed to reach out and find another place that was doing what we wanted, and a successful one. As I thought about how best to tackle this challenge from the city council member, I recalled the people I had met on my journey to bring awareness about Mother 2 Many.

Some time back, I had received the name of a director of a youth shelter in Tacoma. His name was Rick, and he ran a shelter in a residential area. This was important for us because we needed to show the council that there were successful ones running in residential areas and that crime had not gone up because of homeless youth living in the area. I wondered if he would be able to help me with the examples I needed to persuade the rest of the city council in the next big meeting.

I would be seeing Rick on Tuesday. Meeting with new people that work with youth had taught us that there was a huge need for youth shelters, for safe places for our youth to go to, and most of all that youth homelessness is real. Meeting with so many people that are like-minded was encouraging and let us know we were not alone in our thinking. There were very few places that deal with just youth, so meeting others that are like-minded helped us to see a bigger picture, and it also let us know that there is a real need of people that want to help our hurting youth.

Youth are harder to find because they want to fit in; they do not want others to know they are homeless. In all this God would teach us that the way the world thinks of homelessness and how God thinks of homelessness hold two different meanings. God shared with me that just because a youth has a home doesn't mean they are not homeless. What an eye opener for me—just because they have a home doesn't mean they are not homeless. So many youths live in a home but have parents who are not present, sometimes no food, just a covering, but an empty shell of a home.

Deuteronomy 31:8 says, "The LORD himself goes before you and will be with you; he will never leave you nor forsake you. Do not be afraid; do not be discouraged."

As I was praying at my prayer bench, asking God if I was going in the right direction, was I doing what He has called me to do, I realized I'm leading God. I'm sure half the time He was saying, *Joann, what happens when you think you are in control?*

I replied, "Things slow down."

He told me so gently, "So why don't you let me lead? It works out better that way." And then I envision Him giving me a wink and a big smile. He tells me that He loves me, and is so immensely proud of me, that I am His special one. I wish I could tell you that He had the reins again, but I was having troubles giving those back to Him.

While we were waiting on the city council to get back to me on our next meeting, I had other things to prepare for, and one of them was obtaining a 501c3.

One thing we had to have to move forward was our 501c3, and I was very happy that on May 26, 2014, we received an email letting us know that our church would be the covering for our ministry. We could use their 501c3 for year-end tax donations. This was a happy-dance time; this was one step we needed to move forward with a house for the youth. This was a huge weight lifted off my shoulders.

I had tried several times to do my own 501c3. I asked for help and people said yes. They would help but then not come through; or they would help, but it would cost us a lot of money to have them fill out the paperwork. At that time, we did not have the money to file for a 501c3 because there was no money to pay someone to do it, so having our church help us was a huge deal, and we were so very thankful for their help

Money was an issue, and we needed to start earning some to move forward with any plans that we thought were ahead of us. Now that we had a covering of a 501c3, I felt I needed to think about a fundraiser. We needed to start getting money together to be able to buy the building and to show the council that we could pay and be able to sustain ourselves. I thought of the biggest church around, Calvary Community Church, one that was well known in the community. Since we were trying to get money together fast, we needed a fundraiser. Calvary always had fundraisers and events going on. God worked it out that we were able to put a fundraiser together in three weeks.

As I was getting the fundraiser together, I got an email from my church that I needed to get my own 501c3 as soon as possible. I didn't expect this and let Stuart know that I would do my best. My head was spinning, and I was going, *Wow God how in the heck am I going to do all this?* Well in all this, I have found out I work well in pressure situations.

In the meantime, I was able to speak at a couple of Bible study groups. In doing so I met a really nice couple, a retired CPA and his soon-to-be wife, who worked on computers. Thankfully they both loved what God was calling us to do, and they wanted to help. He worked with us on the details for the 501c3 and didn't charge for his time; she made a fundraiser PowerPoint. I had been praying for help with the 501c3, and God brought me a couple who wanted to give back to the community, and M2M fit right in with what they wanted to help with. Both their strengths were my weaknesses, and I was so very thankful for their help and that God brought them into my life. Lane and Jean were a true godsend. Seeing how God worked this out was the best thing, but what was even better was that we knew without a doubt He was in the middle of the situation. Romans 8:28 says, "And we know that in all things God works for the good of those who love him, who have been called according to his purpose."

Two weeks before the fundraiser, a lady at church came up to me and said she wanted to help me get things together. I had shared at a Bible study she had attended, and since we were doing this fundraiser in three weeks' time, it was good to have someone know what to do since this was my first fundraiser. When her daughter was in high school and in cheerleading, she had been the coordinator for getting the fundraiser put together. I had never put a fundraiser together and had no clue of what to do. With her help, my prayers were answered.

Things were coming together, moving much better with all this help, instead of me doing it on my own. God knew I needed help and didn't have a clue in what to do, and He brought me some really great helpers I was doing a lot of things that I knew nothing about, and He was working in and through each situation.

As I knelt in front of my prayer bench at the end of the day, I looked out at the backyard trees, something I did often to just listen to God or just to be silent. God used the trees to speak to me. The branches appeared to be waving at me, winking, and being silly. By that I knew my Father was close with me, that He did not want me to be dismayed or discouraged. He wanted me to let go and let Him have control.

Nothing is impossible for God, and when we are walking with Him, nothing will stop what He has planned. It is so wonderful to know that we are on the right side, and when God has called you into His plan, it will all fall into place at just the right time. He was providing for us financially, and He gave us the people to help work alongside us in M2M at the times we needed help or encouragement. He continued to bring in more for M2M, and He wasn't stopping anytime soon.

Even though I had the fundraiser pieces coming together, I was still waiting for the larger meeting with the city council—and that gave me the butterflies, yet I rested in God's timing and in His way. He had brought our work on Mother 2 Many this far; He would not let us down.

Dear Father, I come to You and ask for strength as I move deeper into Your plan, and I remember nothing is impossible for You. In Jesus's name, amen.

CHAPTER 9

When God Shows Up, You Can Do All Things through Him

For nothing will be impossible with God.

Luke 1:37 ESV

The day dawned bright as I talked with God at my prayer bench. We talked about a lot of things: plans for the fundraiser, the people who were helping run everything, and my ever-present fears and frustrations with the tiny details of this whole process. I was not good with details.

Even though our brochures had been designed, I wanted them updated and asked the friend who had designed them if she could help out again.

To my delight she was very excited to help. We met for lunch to discuss what needed to go on the brochure. I wanted our needs and vision to be really clear for the people who would come to the fundraiser.

As we left the meeting, I was pleased to see how God was continually working each piece and setting every detail in place.

I had another meeting that day with everyone helping out with the fundraiser. But forty-five minutes before the meeting, I received a call from the lady in charge of organizing the fundraiser meeting.

"I'm so sorry, Joann, but I can't make the meeting tonight. I had an allergic reaction to something I ate. I'm in bed and feel awful."

Saddened but not deterred, I asked E, the lady who was to help me with the fundraiser, what I needed to do since she was unable to come to my home. She told me to write up a list of all the things that needed to be done and delegate. As I met with about five ladies, all from my church, we brainstormed everything we felt we needed and who we thought could help in each area. We needed desserts, paper plates, plasticware, coffee, tea, water, centerpieces, and raffle items. And we needed a speaker. Each person picked something they could help with, and then I could breathe a bit.

Over the next four days, I tried to contact E, but with no luck. I was so tensed and stressed my shoulders hurt. She was the one I felt knew everything that needed to be done. She had done fundraisers many times before; I had never done one. By Saturday, a week before the fundraiser, I decided she must not want to do this and emailed her to release her from helping.

But I realized that I had made some assumptions, which I quickly dismissed. I called and found out that she was having an issue with her phone, and that the emails I had sent Wednesday and Thursday did not get to her until Sunday. Sounds like the enemy was trying to stop God's plans. I was so glad that we were able to talk—she was feeling better now and ready to get back on board. I knew that everything would fall into place now.

Also, that morning before the Saturday church meeting, I kept hearing about Jeff, who had a wonderful testimony. I emailed him and asked him if he would speak at the fundraiser. When I got home from the meeting, a voicemail from Jeff was waiting for me. He would speak at our fundraiser. What a great blessing to have him come and share. Everything was coming together!

Sunday morning at church, Steve and I received a word from a dear friend, Jon. After church we always fellowship with friends. When Jon gave Steve and me this word, once again, the tears begin to flow. *Why does God love me so much that He is always encouraging me? I'm not someone important, I'm just me, but yet, He is always letting me know that I'm not far from His thoughts.*

We are in a boat. The waves are coming and hitting the boat, yet we are to stand firm. The wind that is hitting the boat is God. The wind is God! But do not bail, do not bail. Because help will come to us from people we do not expect, and people we expect to help will not help.

I will not bail; I will stand firm because God has asked me to. There are times when I ask myself what am I doing thinking of having a home for youth, talking to city officials, putting a fundraiser together, becoming a nonprofit—this is hard work. There are times I wanted life to be simple again like it was before all this, when I went to work, came home, and nothing else was happening, we had a little bit of stress, and planned for retirement someday soon. Even with those thoughts, I would keep going, doing what my Father has asked.

And then I was reminded of what I was told some months ago: *We will have people for a season, and people we do not expect will join us*, and that started to happen. There have been those who I thought would help, but they are having nothing to do with our ministry, and people I did not expect are on board 100 percent. God is our teacher. He is our provider, and He is a huge encourager. Every step is with Him, for we are not alone.

It was Monday, and time to go into town and try to get donations for the fundraiser in a few days. My friend Sue felt that God had told her to help me, so we headed down to Sumner and got five businesses to help. This was a huge blessing. I would not have gone if she hadn't gone with me, and God knew that! So thankful for dear friends.

It was Wednesday night and our last meeting before our fundraiser. We had a small group, and after a few errands we would be done. I was so relieved that everything was falling into place for our fundraiser. We had ten days to prepare, and it was so amazing how God brought good people in to help me. God's hand was in everything.

The day before the fundraiser, I received an email that our speaker was sick and might not be able to speak. Then another email that the person who would be opening up in prayer would not be able to attend because he must work. Then a third email from a volunteer bringing the laptop who was sick. I wondered what the heck was going on.

I was just starting to feel discouraged, but then I remembered that the door was open for us to have the fundraiser. Steve and I began praying about the situation, and God intervened. I would share more about Mother 2 Many. A friend was able to bring a laptop.

And to my surprise, Jeff was able to speak even though he did not feel good. What a blessing! His testimony was right along the lines of where God was leading us, working with youth, and I was excited to hear what he had to say. He had been on drugs and homeless, and one day he went to a Celebrate Recovery meeting, and his life began to change. Today he owns an automotive repair shop, is happily married, and has a beautiful daughter.

All because someone came alongside him and said, *Hey, you matter. Let's get help.*

We got to the church, and volunteers were already there. The place looked huge, and I wondered if we could make it all look wonderful. Well, by the time the tables were all set, the raffle items were in place, and all the desserts were there, the place looked like pros had decorated.

Then it was time for people to come. Slowly they came in. We had fifteen tables ready; seven were filled. Volunteers sat at the other tables. The evening went very well and smoothly, and everyone had fun. All the raffle items went, no desserts were left, and we made enough to pay for our 501c3. The extra money paid for the fundraiser and even some extra! God is good!

I was saddened, though, by the lack of people who attended because I wanted more people to see the need for our youth. But the next day, I received several emails that changed how I felt.

The first one:

I just wanted to thank you for tonight and let you know that I'm here to serve in any way I can. I know you were able to plant a lot of seeds tonight, and I am excited to see what God will do in the coming months!

The second one:

While the numbers weren't quite what you were expecting, don't be discouraged. For that evening, those that were supposed to be there were. I was impressed with the number of volunteers you had supporting this. I know things happen behind the scenes, but if you were a guest it seemed to go without a hitch. You and Jeff, the speaker, were very thorough and did a wonderful job sharing. The auctioneer was great and your volunteers were terrific.

Those two emails that really touched my heart and I was so thankful to have friends who write such nice things and who are such a great support system. Seeds were planted, what God wanted to do, so how could I argue with God. This was His show, and I was here to do what He asked. God was using others to be seed planters. I would be reminded of this a few years later, and as Galatians 6:9 says, "Let us not become weary in doing good, for at the proper time we will reap a harvest if we do not give up."

On Saturday, we went to a prayer meeting. I loved these meetings, for God moves so strongly here. One of the ladies brought me a small bag of clothes, and I wanted to cry. God had told her to go find some clothes to give to me for the youth. It was His way of encouraging me. And then I received an email from another friend:

That is funny you mention someone donating clothes. It has been on my heart for several days (really since the auction) to donate several youth and adult sized sweatshirts. I did not want you to be bombarded with a giant heavy box of sweatshirts, but I am ready to hand them off when you need them! God bless you for all you do and you're right, God is taking care of the details!

God was taking care of all the details. He was teaching me, bringing people into my life to start building relationships, and opening doors for me that would help me later.

Dear heavenly Father, You know that we need helpers, and we ask that You bring us the right ones at the right time, and that they will have Your heart. Give us discernment to help us in these times. In Jesus's name, amen.

CHAPTER 10

When the Walls Come Crashing Down

And we know that in all things God works for the good of those
who love him, who have been called according to his purpose.

Romans 8:28 NKJV

The week after the fundraiser, I received a call. Reverend Tom wanted to meet with me about possible investors who might be interested in what we were doing. While I was excited, I tried to keep that excitement on low volume. I wanted to hear what God had to say before the excitement started.

I met with Rev. Tom who has a lot of energy. He shared that he has done a lot of things with youth. He had worked with Teen Challenge for young adult men and was excited about Mother 2 Many. Because of his involvement with Teen Challenge, he knew a lot of people who could possibly help us with funding. He had a lot of questions. He wanted to know our vision, what our plans were for the youth we wanted to house, where did we want to house them, how far along were we, and other questions. I felt confident in my answers, but as he looked on intently, I wasn't sure if he was totally confident in my answers.

I truly hoped Rev. Tom was the person who would help us get going. We needed to have investors because the St. Andrew building was going to cost us a million dollars. Rev. Tom knew how to run a home for youth but didn't know any investors. I needed investors before we went in front of the council members. Things were not looking good. Once again, I left disappointed and feeling discouraged. But I was not giving up. God wanted me to work with youth; I just needed to find my way and see where He wanted me. Though I was more determined to get the ball rolling, I wanted it to roll in the right direction.

My brain was working overtime as I tend to get myself in the way when I start to overthink things. Writing has helped me get back on track to be able to hear what God was saying.

The next day I sent out emails asking for prayer about a new building that someone had brought to my attention. It was an old retirement home in a rundown part of town. But a few of my intercessor friends told me not to focus on this. One of them felt it was the enemy coming in to take the prayer away from our upcoming meeting with the council to get approval for the new zoning for the St. Andrews building. So I emailed everyone back and asked them to focus on the meeting for Monday. Having people who pray was so important and was a great way to keep me on track for what God wants us to do. The enemy did not want this to happen, and I would always need people to come alongside me and pray!

Our second meeting with the city council was on Monday.

As I prepared, I read a page of an old devotional, *Women's Devotional New Testament with Psalms & Proverbs*. I received devotionals each day from Proverbs 31, and sometimes I did not have time to read them, so I read them whenever I did have time. This was one of those days. As I was reading, I wondered if I was doing everything right. Was I the right person to be entrusted to take care of teens? I wanted to do everything right, but it didn't seem like I was. I wanted to please God in everything I did, and I just didn't want to mess things up. The devotional spoke of hearing from God, to be reassured by His words, and to know that He sees me. Reading this devotional, I knew

God heard me, He saw me, and most of all He knew that I would do the best job I can because He chose me!

Our Father is forever an encourager, and He never leaves us alone. He holds our hands most of the time and carries us when we truly think we can do no more. He is right there with us, and He will never leave us nor forsake us! Thank You, Father, for Your words of encouragement, for Your love, and for never leaving me.

Monday arrived. Steve and I met with the council, and though it was a little discouraging, we knew that our big God would work things out the way He wanted them to work out, which sometimes is not what we have envisioned. There were three councilmembers who said no; one said this whole idea was just overwhelming; two really did not say anything; and one was totally on our side. The police chief did not see the need for a teen home and was keeping the interest of his community a top priority.

I was discouraged, mad, and very much disheartened. I left the meeting feeling defeated, but tried to keep my head up, knowing that all would work out just the way God intended. I would keep trying. Another meeting was set up for some time soon. I would be talking one on one with only a few of the council members, and that might be better.

On Sunday, Pastor gave a sermon that touched both Steve and me. There were things God was saying. *The money will come. Persevere. Do not give up, do be quiet, and just stand strong.*

On Monday, I met with two more ladies who wanted to help us. One was a grant writer and the other had a lot of experience in fundraising, both of which I knew nothing about, so this was a huge addition to our team. What a joy to know there are people who love to put fundraisers together, and they do it well, and grant writing—that was truly a blessing. Once again, God was bringing me the best, and that was the neatest thing of all.

Wednesday night, I received a phone call from one of the neighbors of the old St. Andrews building we were looking to purchase. He was a Seattle police officer and dealt with homeless teens, and he had some concerns and wanted to meet and discuss them. I was excited for this because it was the first neighbor to call. This could give us a chance to really talk to him about what we would like to see happen. We met at a local hamburger place, and he brought his wife. We sat at a booth and then introduced ourselves.

The meeting did not turn out the way I expected. Being a cop's kid, I could understand how he and his wife must have felt. He had dealt with homeless youth, he saw the worst of these kids, and he didn't want to have this type of youth in his neighborhood, a neighborhood that had families and was pretty quiet. What we wanted to do, he felt, was change that. Then he gave me six pages of questions. As I read them, a bunch were repeated two or three times. When we left, I was exhausted.

The next day as Steve and I talked, I realized it was a good thing that the neighbor had asked all those questions. I needed to know the answers to those questions, so I made appointments with people I had already talked with to have them help with all the questions. I asked the police officer neighbor if he would give me some time to find the answers, which he said was fine. That was good, because a day or two was not enough time to answer all those questions. Plus, nothing was really happening with the council meeting being set up, so the next step was for me to pay for a permit for the zoning of the St. Andrew building, and stand in front of a council once more for approval. The $1000 permit was nonrefundable. I needed to convince the council that having a home for homeless youth was a good idea and that we were not bringing in every bad youth who lived in Washington.

So in preparing to answer the questions, I met with Joe, a young man who oversaw a youth center in Auburn. Joe was a young man with a great smile and a love for the youth in his area. Joe had been working with youth for a few years and knew of the huge need for a place for homeless youth to stay. He also had a lot of information, and I appreciated what he had for me. I learned from Joe the laws concerning youth moving into a home without living with their parents; they must have a letter of parental consent. Also, nonprofits do not have all the same rules as others do, but in running a home, you have to have a full staff with someone there twenty-four seven. There were a lot more details to having a home for homeless than what I had imagined. I needed to know all the details about running a home.

Next I met with Brian, who worked at an emergency five-person shelter in Olympia. Brian was a young man in his early thirties who also had a hard life growing up, and it was his turn to help those that needed it. He had a lot of good information and even sent me their daily structured schedule for their youth, which is important in these young people's lives. They had school for them and helped them find work to get them on the right track. Brian told me that he totally supported us and would help us if we needed anything. It was great to hear the positivity and it gave me the push I needed!

Some of the other questions that this couple gave us were law enforcement questions. There was one officer in Puyallup I could talk to. We set up a meeting for the next week. I also called another shelter in Seattle, which we went to. Also, we met another friend who helped the homeless and a young man named Chris from the Seattle Gospel Mission. It seemed things were falling into place, and that was a relief. Meeting with each of these different organizations was really helpful to us to see what all was entailed in having a home for youth.

Sunday at church, I received a word from a friend telling me that God knows what we are going through. Remember, He is with us. I had no idea how much I needed to hear her words until the next day.

Monday night, I checked my emails to find another request from the neighbor we had met with. This time he sent thirty pages of questions, which he had also sent to the city council. He said it was my responsibility to answer the questions to put the other neighbors at ease. I went upstairs to my office, clenching my fists. This was getting to be a real nightmare, and I needed to sit down, calm myself, and regroup.

Thank goodness, I was getting ready to meet with other friends to discuss the other questions. My friends gave me a lot to laugh about, and I just love them. To my amazement, one of them took the sixteen condensed pages and answered some of the questions for me. What a blessing she was, and again I was so very thankful.

On Tuesday, I met with the chief of Puyallup. He was very encouraging and let me know that he was there to help if needed. He also gave me some great input on answering the questions, and that was encouraging, something I needed badly.

Now that I had all the answers to the questions, I sent them to the council and to the neighbor who had sent them. I also had sent an email to one of the councilmen, asking if he would like to meet some of the youth. I wanted him to see that there was a need.

Later, to my total shock, I received this email from one of the council members. He told me that he loved what we were doing, but (that word that no one likes) he couldn't support what we wanted to do. He wished us the best of luck in wherever God was taking us.

After reading, I cried. I cried hard. I cried a bucket of tears. This was a hit in the gut. I asked God, "What am I doing wrong? Am I not doing what you asked?" I needed to know He was there and that He was listening. And He was right there, as always, and He heard my prayers. He had given me the right people to come in and help when I felt discouraged.

My friend Tina was one of them. That was what I needed. I called her, and we talked for forty-five minutes. She told me, "When you start to feel overwhelmed, just imagine what Noah was thinking when God told him to build this enormous ark with rudimentary hand tools. Noah did it. You can too." By the time we were done, I prayed for her, which helped me feel better. I knew this was just another bump in the road, but was it? Was I truly going in the right direction, or was I once again leading God instead of Him leading me? God had a vision of what He wanted, and my vision was getting a little distorted.

Even with the answer from the one council member, I was glad that I had sent all the answered questions to the council and to the neighborhood man who sent them. I felt that it was out of respect for the man and woman who took all that time to write them. I didn't know if one day I would run into them again, and I wanted it to be on

WHEN THE WALLS COME CRASHING DOWN

good terms; his questions were important, and so were his concerns. Plus, their questions helped me to see and look at what I was wanting to do, and it was a little bit out of my league. There was a lot I didn't know, and a lot I hadn't really thought of, and their questions helped me see that, maybe not at first but over time.

I felt this door was closing. Even though the door had been closed to St. Andrews, and God had been having a dear friend send me word after word of encouragement, I was filled to the brim, and it was amazing. His words encouraged me to not give up, to keep going, that God was on our side, and He had big plans for us. We just needed to be patient.

We knew we were going to have to fight for this, or maybe I needed to see the bigger picture. God was closing doors on the drop-in center and the house, but I was not totally seeing it. And it took some time to really see, but I finally did. I finally realized that my vision was just that, my vision. I had let too many others plant seeds about a home for the homeless that I lost sight of where God was truly taking us. It was not having a home for the youth, and it was not having a drop-in center either. It was much bigger than that. I was about to see where God wanted us.

Dear heavenly Father, help me keep my eyes on You. Help me not to stuff You in a box, but to recognize Your plans are the best plans. I just must be patient. In Jesus's name, amen.

CHAPTER 11

When God Uses Others to Put You on the Right Path

I sought the Lord, and he answered me; he
delivered me from all my fears.

Psalm 34:44 NKJV

It was the week of August 11, 2014. Even with the councilman not supporting us, I remembered that when a door closes, I should not try to open it. Over the next few months, I started to see the bigger picture. It would be God who made things happen. The door to the house—*my* vision—had closed.

Life moved forward, and I was looking forward to seeing where God really wanted us to be. I had a few meetings, along with two of my favorite times of prayer this week. I attended the Puyallup Homeless Coalition meeting. One thing resonated with me when one of the members said, "Do these people realize that what we are doing is not what we want to see happen, but what God wants?" A little over a year ago, I thought I would be working still at a job I did not really like and waiting to retire with Steve, but instead God had a different plan. This was His plan, not mine.

I then had a meeting with a supervisor at Coffee Oasis. They are the only other faith-based shelter around that houses youth for a longer period of time. Speaking with the people at Coffee Oasis helped me understand homeless youth much better. I learned that youth simply want to be loved and treated well and have experienced a lot of hurt in the course of their young lives. I also learned that to help the youth well, it was important to show up for them consistently. What you do and say truly matter in these kids' lives. It's good to give them the hope that they need.

On Sunday, I received a wonderful revelation from God. Last week, I was reading John 15:15: "I no longer call you servants, because a servant does not know his master's business. Instead, I have called you friends, for everything that I learned from my Father I have made known to you." That verse came to life to me, and it was the start of a relationship with God. I was learning to let down those guarded walls and relax with my heavenly Father. After church, I said, "Thank you, Father and friend," and He said to me, "You finally got it." Yes, I finally got it. After fifty-four years, I'm so glad I finally got that He is my dearest friend. Then after church, I received a late birthday card and a word from my friend:

> I'll never leave or abandon you [He has told me this since I was little; this is very dear to me]. You can count on my goodness and my mercy every day of your life. I love you and will always keep my life-giving promises to you. When you are faithful under trial, you'll receive a crown of life from me. Anticipating the day when you'll dwell with Me forever. Eternally your loving Father God and friend.

I never told my friend about what revelation God had given me, so when I read this card, I cried. Friend, He is my friend, my daddy, my everything. Wow, that is the best thing ever. It wasn't about religion; it was about having a relationship with our heavenly Father that is so different from our relationship with our earthly father. My relationship with God had really changed, and by that relationship growing, my relationship with my own dad was changing. Hurts were being healed, and all because I had said yes to God.

One thing I love about how God works is that He encourages. Steve and I went to the Kingdom Congress meeting, an amazing ministry that is trying to get the churches to be in prayer twenty-four seven every day of the month through fasting and prayer. Since starting Mother 2 Many, God has shown me the importance of fasting. I have fasted many times and heard from God. At the beginning of the meeting, we got a word from a friend that God was going to "catapult" us. I had heard a lot of words on this, so it was a confirmation.

Then at the end of the night, we were asked to pray with three to four other people. Steve prayed with the man in front of us, and the woman prayed for both Steve and me. She began her prayer about us being in a ministry, and I laughed silently because she did not know we were already in ministry. And then she told us that we were going to be detoured and taken in a direction we knew nothing about. God was going to get things going because of the urgency of what was happening in the world.

This gave us so much hope and excitement. I had learned much in the past few months, healing from past hurts, learning that Jesus wants to be our friend, and that having a relationship with our heavenly Father is changing us. What God has for us is something we know nothing about, but He is with us, guiding and directing us, even if we have to take a detour. He is there. What lies ahead will be simply amazing.

Dear heavenly Father, I give thanks to You for teaching me and for not giving up on me, even when I take a wrong turn. Thank You for being an amazing God who loves His kids. In Jesus's name, amen.

CHAPTER 12

Sometimes God Has a Few Detours

*Jesus replied, "You do not realize now what I am
doing, but later you will understand."*

John 13:7

I'm so glad that God doesn't give up on us even when we go into
the wrong direction. Everything works for the glory of God, and
it was time to go a different direction.

Some time ago I had the honor to meet an amazing young man
who worked for Seattle Union Gospel Mission. He contacted me about
meeting a woman who holds prayer meetings in Tukwila and said
that I should talk to her about our vision. At first, I wasn't sure why,
but when I met up with Jenny, I understood. Jenny loved her community. She has that spunky personality of being a fighter. Her church
is right in the middle of an area that is very poor, a lot of immigrants,
a low-income community. We talked, and I shared again our vision.
She invited us to her prayer meeting.

There were about ten people at this meeting, including one of
the school board members. I shared my vision with the group. She
was excited to hear where our hearts were. As we talked, she shared
that they used to have a backpack program at Thorndyke Elementary,
and it would be great to start it up again. Though she did not speak
directly to us, my little brain started working once we left the meeting.
I began to think about the words I had received weeks before and how
it seemed to be fitting together.

Was this where God was leading us? I knew nothing about putting backpacks together for youth, yet I could learn. Was this where our help would come from? So many questions, but I was ready to hear and see what God had in store for us. Her prayer touched me. She had prayed, that we will go wherever He asks, that we will always say yes. God knows our hearts, and He knows we will do His will, not ours. We are not afraid because He is leading. God is so good. He is always with us, and always encouraging us.

The next day I then decided to email Jenny, asking her what we could do. She responded right away:

> So glad you contacted me. It is very timely. I was wondering if there would be any way you could possibly meet with me next Friday, August 29 at 2:30 p.m.? I have a meeting scheduled with Chris of UGM [Union Gospel Mission] and Mary of Tukwila Schools to discuss this very issue. The numbers just came in on our district, and over 11 percent of our students are homeless. We want to strategize how to mobilize the body of Christ around this issue. Perhaps you have some insights that could help us.

This was exciting, and of course I told her yes, we would be there, but in the meantime I got some very exciting news. Tuesday, August 26, 2014, I went to the post office and found a letter from the IRS making Mother 2 Many officially a 501c3! It had taken less than forty days to be approved. When I have been told it could take up to six months to a year to be approved, God had done it in less than forty days. I love when God shows off! We no longer needed our church to be a covering over M2M; we were on our own.

We had the chance to meet with Jenny, Chris, and one of the school board members who shared what we would like to help them with. They were all excited to get working on the backpack program. But this was also something that would take time. We started contacting people to help. We needed food supplies and we needed permission, so we set up meetings with Thorndyke's principal.

With this all happening fast, I didn't think about the disappointment of not being able to have a home for youth, but once it came back to my thoughts, God always brought someone to give me encouragement. A friend emailed me, and it touched me very deeply because it showed that God had not given up on us, even though I had been going in the wrong direction. Here is her email:

One thing I have been waiting to share with you for an awhile. If you have not already heard this, it's the story of Joseph. God gave Joseph a vision of what He wanted to do with Joseph. Joseph was happy and excited so he went and shared it with his brothers, thinking they would be excited with him. But look at the steps that took to the fulfillment of his vision.
He was then thrown into a pit
He was sold as a slave
He worked for someone else
He was falsely accused of rape
He was thrown into prison
He was forgotten in prison
Finally, when God was ready, God exalted him to be second in the land.
That is not the path we want to take but, normally when we receive God's vision for our life, we are not ready for it and God has to take us through several steps to get us ready. Also, these steps are not ones that we want but they are necessary for us to get where God is taking us. The vision for our life is to help us endure the preparation that it will take. At the beginning, when God gives us His vision for our lives, we typically want to use God to bring that vision to pass. We are the master, and He is our servant. God must take us through a process to turn that around. Once we become

His servant wanting to follow Him wherever He takes us with our servant's heart, then God can do some really great things through us without it wrecking us.

I see that you are in this process. Submit to it no matter how long it takes, and you will be amazed at where God takes you!

Yes, we were in the process, and yes, we were becoming the servant. I didn't quite know that yet, but we were becoming who God was preparing us to be. In the Bible, Joseph also misinterpreted his vision, but he finally came around, and God did something amazing in his life. It is important to not give up, to keep pushing forward no matter what. In the end it is so worth it. You will see that from the very start God was there, and you had to go through what you went through to get to your destination. All the good and bad make you into who you were meant to be.

Sunday morning we listened to a pastor share on Joseph. This really spoke to me and tied all this together. The Scripture is for today just as much as it was for yesterday and many years ago. The Bible is our guide to life; it is our food, inspiration, and words from our Father. You will always read and understand something new!

As I waited for our meeting with Jenny, Chris, and the school board member, I went to my regular prayer circle. There were a lot of people there and a few new ladies I had not met before. As we introduced ourselves, I shared what we felt God was preparing us for, working with homeless youth, and we continued with prayer.

At the end of session, one of the ladies I just met opened up to me and started to share with me that she was homeless as a teen. We were seated in big, comfy chairs in an open room but in a quiet corner. She was a petite woman in her fifties with a kind face and soft voice. The sun was shining in the window, giving warmth and a shine to her face. As she spoke, she had a sadness, and was almost a little embarrassed about what she was going to share about her time of being homeless.

She lived in Sumner in the early seventies, and homelessness was something you never heard of back then, or maybe it was called a different name. Her home life was not good. Her parents were abusive, and drugs seemed to be more important than their daughter. She felt the only way out was to leave. She wanted to continue going to the same school, and she wanted to make sure she had a future, so that meant staying in Sumner. The only place she could find to sleep safely was in a chicken coop. Washington is cold and rainy during the fall and winter months, so sleeping there was not the warmest or best place for a young girl. She shared with a close friend what she was doing, and the friend's family let her stay with them ever so often. She was able to shower at school.

A happy day came when she finally got to live with a family, one that was loving, caring, and gave her a taste of a real family. One thing she shared that meant the world to her was that this family sat together for dinner, which she had never experienced before. But then one day, because of state laws, the state got involved, and she went from foster home to foster home. Her life was hard, but she finished school and did not follow in her parents' footsteps. At the time we talked, she was happily married, a mother and grandmother, and her life was good. She gave all the credit to her relationship with Jesus, He helped her through all the stuff she had to go through.

Hearing her story really tugged at my heart and encouraged me not to give up and to continue the path that God had for us. No youth needed to live this way.

Since meeting with Chris, Jenny, and others and hearing their stories, I realized God was moving us in a different direction. Was it the backpack program or something else? Once again it was important to fast. I had been fasting for almost three weeks. I took one day a week and slept in. I had to because if I didn't, my body just did not respond like I wanted. But I continued fasting.

> *I realized for so long it was all about religion and not about a relationship.*

God has brought a lot to me in times of fasting. Waiting on Him is probably one of the hardest things for me to do. But I believe this time is a time to be in my word, to be in prayer, and to just take time to be with Him. Before, my prayers were ten to fifteen minutes. Now, they are one hour in the morning, and I try to talk with Him throughout the day. My relationship with Him has grown so much. I realized for so long it was all about religion and not about a relationship. God wanted to have that with me, and because of this walk, He was getting just that. What a wonderful thing to finally be free to love your heavenly Father and to be loved back.

God wants to have a strong relationship with each of us, and it is so important to let Him in and to share all we are with Him. We are important to Him. Friends like to spend time with each other, and God wants our friendship.

It was September 2014, and we didn't think about a home for youth, but we thought about what would be next. From January 2013 until now, God healed many hurts, broke down walls, taught us about homelessness, grew us, and grew our relationship with Him, teaching us patience, to have love for the broken, to rely on Him for all things and so much more. I was in awe of what God had done and was continuing to do in our lives. Our journey in becoming Mother 2 Many was about to really start.

Dear heavenly Father, thank You so much for believing in me. Thank You for walking me through each area and teaching me about what You were getting us ready to do. Thank You! In Jesus's name, amen.

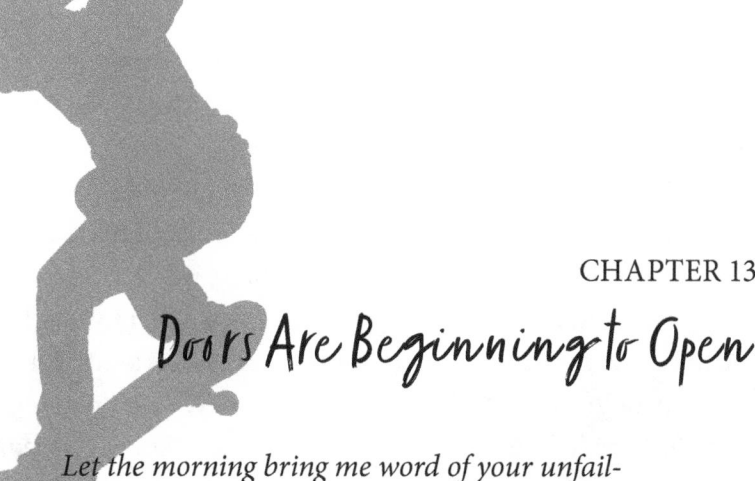

CHAPTER 13

Doors Are Beginning to Open

Let the morning bring me word of your unfail-
ing love, for I have put my trust in you. Show me the
way I should go, for to you I entrust my life.

Psalm 143:8

In October 2014, God brought the skate park back to the forefront. It seems that we had taken a detour away from where God really wanted us to go, which was the skate park. Steve and I met with a good friend with whom we prayed, and she gave us a word that confirmed that we were to go to Sumner Skate Park to reach youth in our area. My heart started to beat wildly, and tears began to form in my eyes. It had been twenty-one months since He had given me the words, *You will help homeless teens.* I had so many questions running through my mind. I asked, "Lord, do we really get to start helping your kids?"

I was so excited; it was happy-dance time. God knew we would finally get back to where He wanted us to be, the skate park. So now we prepared. I set a date of the first week in December to be at the skate park. We had things to do. The backpacks were the first items to be filled, and we decided on these: nonperishable food items, toiletry items, hats, gloves, and the Book of John. Next I needed to have something to hand out to the kids when they came up to the table.

Steve and I had met Rudy, a youth pastor, at a ministry luncheon months back, and he was on board to help us get the word out and helped us decide what we needed to start with. As we sat at his home, his wife, Sarah, was there to join us. These two love youth, and had a youth group that meets at their home. Rudy was a big kid himself, which made him the perfect person to help us start this new journey of feeding the youth in need in the Sumner area. Rudy was a skate-boarder, had his own long board, and was excited to go to the park and skate. Rudy's and Sarah's two daughters were also eager to help. As we sat on the couch discussing what we wanted to do, the excite-ment was very much present in this room that has seen a lot of youth come through their doors. It was nice to have this amazing family come alongside and help us. Their teen daughters were amazing in helping with their input. We decided to start with granola bars, hot chocolate, juice, water, and hats and gloves. Our plan would be to do this once a week and try to reach these youth.

A lot had happened in the past three weeks. God had confirmed repeatedly that the skate park was where we were to go. Having some-one share with me what God was saying really helped to confirm that, especially when it was someone that had no idea of who we were and what God had called us to do. At my Kingdom Culture class I was taking, they had a prayer time where they brought a team of people from another church, and they spoke over each person in the class and prayed over each of us. This was something they had all been trained to do, listening to God's voice.

This special time was called Original Design. I had never done one of these, so it was really different. But I was excited to see what this was all about and to hear what complete strangers had to say, but what I heard was even more exciting. Two people prayed with me or for me. We were in a circle. They were all in front of me in this circle, and we had a nice distance away from other groups that were doing the same way, so it was more private. We were all sitting in chairs that are metal with soft cushions, and the circle was tight. As we were sitting there for a few minutes, they started to pray and they started to write down what they felt God was telling them about me. As each one felt they have heard everything, they stopped and waited for the others to also finish. Then one by one they shared what God had given them.

The first one to speak over me was a woman, probably in her forties, with dark hair, a soft voice, and a sweet face. As she spoke to me, she looked directly into my eyes and said, "You have a mother's heart."

Now what is a mother's heart? To me it is a mom that loves unconditionally, is always there, laughs with you, cries with you, and is your biggest cheerleader. Someone who will never leave you when things get tough. Someone who stands up for you no matter what.

Wow, a mother's heart—that is what God is saying I have. I looked at her with a smile on my face and joy in my heart. Then she continued to share: "loves children, loves to worship, peace maker, child faith." This was what God told me at the very beginning of this when I was going to quit my job. Then she shared this: She saw a picture of God and His hand reaching out for me. He wants me to depend more on Him, and not so much on me. I am trying every day, but I will try harder. He is patient with me, and He will help me to overcome this.

The next was another woman, a bit younger, who had done this a bit longer than the other one. You could tell by her confidence in what she shared and she was eager to share what God had told her to share with me: *People really trust you because of your nonjudgmental, grateful, and thankful heart. You see the best in all people.* Then she read this verse from Luke 4:18–19:

The Spirit of the Lord is on me, because he has anointed me to proclaim good news to the poor. He has sent me to proclaim freedom for the prisoners and recovery of the sight for the blind, to set the oppressed free.
To proclaim the year of the Lord's favor.
You seek the lonely and forgotten, caregiver, not afraid to care, very kind approachable you are a people's safe place.

Then Psalm 23. A Psalm of David.

The Lord is my shepherd, I lack nothing.
He makes me lie down in green pastures; he leads me beside
quiet waters,
He refreshes my soul. He guides me along the right paths
for his name's sake.
Even though I walk through the darkest valley, I will fear
no evil, for you are with me; your rod and your staff, they
comfort me.
You prepare a table before me in the presence of my enemies.
You anoint my head with oil; my cup overflows.
Surely your goodness and love will follow me all the days
of my life, and I will dwell in the house of the Lord forever.

She told me that God had given her those verses for me to read. "You would get down and dirty for God, heart of a missionary, wherever He sends you, you would go. Mentor to many, wisdom with understanding, timing, at just the right time, creative, support, good listener, slow to speak," and then she saw me sitting in a big chair, meditating.

The last person to give me a word was a man. This is what God shared with him: "Not easily swayed, you decide on the issue and know where you stand and do not veer to the right or to the left. You love God and seek ways to go deeper into Him, pillar to your community or peers. I see you struggling with a perplexing issue, and God wants to let you know how much he loves you and your heart for Him. There is victory!"

In hearing these amazing words, I was so encouraged to move forward. With each of these words, God was sharing how He felt about me and that He believed in me. I needed to believe in myself. I believed then I could go forward and do what God has called me to do, and that I could do so without fear, without doubt, and with confidence knowing that He is with me. He has opened my eyes to see the hurting. He has taken those blinders off, and opened my heart to love those who seem to be forgotten.

Dear heavenly Father, thank You for leading me in this direction. Thank You for trusting me with Your children. Help me to keep my eyes on You and only You. In Jesus's name, amen.

CHAPTER 14

Excited for Our New Journey: Feeding God's Children

*He answereth and saith unto them, He that hath
two coats, let him impart to him that hath none;
and he that hath meat, let him do likewise.*

Luke 3:11 KJV

On December 1, 2014, the week before we started at the skate park, Jenny, Steve, and I finally met with the Tukwila school principal. He was an older man in his fifties, with dark hair, a small frame, and a kind face that showed his worries and concerns for the students. He was eager to hear what we would like to do for his students, and we were eager to share with him. After about thirty minutes, he was completely on board.

We are all thrilled, and we planned to start by the first of 2015. We split up the responsibilities. As we were talking, I remembered a pastor I had met at a nonprofit conference about six month ago who had a big church in Tukwila. When I got home from the our meeting, I found his card and made a call to see if he would be interested in meeting so I could share with him what we were starting up in his neighborhood, and he said yes.

Jenny organized with others to put donation boxes at their churches or in nearby stores. Several churches helped with a food drive. Now it was time to get things ready at the school. We were able to store our items in the school's utility room. Then we needed bins to separate the items so we could form an assembly line. We were excited when someone donated two hundred backpacks to our program.

The city of Tukwila was near where Steve had grown up, and his little sister had attended Thorndyke. Thorndyke had the highest amount of homeless youth in King County. These were elementary children, and over 80 percent were considered homeless. We served such a diverse group of students, comprised of families where English was their second language and where many families shared rent. Once we started in January, it was great to see the children come into school with joy on their faces. They were excited to be there, and they were excited to get the backpacks each Friday. Both students and parents knew we cared and were there to help.

All our food items were nonperishable and would go home to the youth who needed food for the weekend. We had a list of all the students and who had certain dietary requests. We did have an issue, though; since some of the parents didn't speak or read English, the backpacks didn't always come back to us. So, we would just give them plastic grocery bags, which seemed to work much better.

Steve and I met with the pastor I had met at a nonprofit conference and were able to share with him what we were doing with the backpack program for Thorndyke. He was on board to help. After our talk, he asked that I come and share in front of his mission group. I agreed and spoke in front of about fifty people. I shared our heart for the homeless youth and how starting the backpack program at Thorndyke was the beginning of feeding the youth. After I spoke, a lot of people told us they were glad that we wanted to help their community, and they were excited to partner with us. This church ended up being one of our biggest donors and helped us to make sure our backpacks were always filled. The meeting between the pastor and me as the nonprofit was a divine appointment, there is no doubt. God is always working even when we don't see it.

We did the backpack program for six months and helped the school get things going. But our outreach was to be closer to home.

Helping Tukwila was a blessing and taught us a lot too. Many times I wondered why we started this program, and God showed me once again why. Homelessness does not discriminate. It doesn't care about your age, your race, your religion. Homelessness can hit anyone. God had put us in the street working with homeless people, now at an elementary school, and next a skate park. He was teaching us and showing us that it didn't matter who you were, homelessness is everywhere.

Our time in Tukwila ended in June 2015, and with it came a reimbursement check for fuel for the last six months. God took care of our needs. God had given us a wonderful time and we made new friends, but a backpack program was not meant to be our main focus—the skate park was.

Dear heavenly Father, You know what is coming, and You know what we will face. Help us not to doubt You or question but watch as You put everything into place. Thank You, Father. In Jesus's name, amen!

CHAPTER 15

Going to the Skate Park

And God is able to bless you abundantly, so that in all things at all times, having all that you need, you will abound in every good work.

2 Corinthians 9:8

Before we started the skate park, it seemed that I was constantly trying to figure out if I was doing the right thing, I believe the enemy was coming in and trying to get me not to do what God had asked. Our minds are always a great place to start, and my mind was never quiet, something that did not help. The enemy would throw in doubts and insecurities, but God knew I would overcome those things because He had a plan for my life.

When I was young, the enemy had tried to destroy me many times, from a car accident to almost drowning twice. God's hand had saved me. And later in life, He never let things go too far, keeping me from harm. He had always been there because He had a plan, and no one was going to change that plan. He wanted me to be a Mother 2 Many!

In November 2014, we met up with a wonderful youth pastor, Rudy, who had heard me share at the pastors' meeting a few months back about wanting to start up a skate park outreach. Since the backpack program hadn't started up yet, I could focus on the skate park outreach getting started. I was excited to hear from him since I did not think the pastors wanted to help us. He loved what we wanted to do at the skate park and told us he was a skater, and he, too, had been one of those troubled kids. He wanted to come alongside us and help us get this going. His youth group was on board too. We put fliers up at the skate park, on the grocery store board, and on sidewalk benches.

On November 20, 2014, I got some news that could have upset me. But I guess in a lot of ways, I knew that we were going a different direction from having a home for the teens. I guess in some ways, I still had hope, but this was God's way of saying, *Joann, I have you right where you were supposed to be, at the skate park.* St. Andrews had sold, and I knew then that God was not leading us to have a home for the youth. He had something else in store for us, and without a doubt I knew that it was the skate park. I was being a little stubborn in letting go, but God was saying, *It is time, and do not look back, only forward*, and that is what I have done. I am so thankful I did not defy God. I continued to look forward—something that was hard at times, but so worth it.

I was reminded of the detour God told us about. Well, one day we may come back to having a home for homeless youth, but until then, I just wanted to do what God has called me to do—love His kids, and help the skate park kids.

The day had finally arrived; it was December 8, 2014, and we were going to the skate park. We had our truck ready to go with backpacks of food items to hand out to those in need; a banner letting people know that we were there to offer a hot drink and a snack; a card table; hot chocolate, cups, hot water in thermoses, water and Capri Sun, granola bars, hats and gloves. We were all so excited. The day had finally come to be able to finally go out and meet the youth in our community.

It was a beautiful sunny day in Sumner with a cool breeze on our first fall day at the skate park. The skate park was right next to a baseball field, and an elementary school was just down the road; in fact, they had a walkway from the elementary school right to the Sumner Skate Park. The high school was also about two blocks away. There were apartment buildings across one street and townhouses across another. It had a huge parking lot. Forty or more cars could park there, and the reason for this large parking lot was because of the baseball field. So this gave us plenty of room to set up and not get in anyone's way. St. Andrew's new church was right behind the skate park, and we could see the beautiful gold cross from where we set up.

We arrived with great excitement; butterflies were in our tummies and a hope that we were going to see a lot of youth. We set up the card table with granola bars, juice, water, hats, gloves, and hot chocolate, which took about five minutes, but that was OK, we were ready. We had a great turnout of volunteers; we had eight volunteers. One of our volunteers, our wonderful youth pastor Rudy, was skating on his skateboard. He had a long board and was having way too much fun, but it got the kids' attention as they were walking home from school. As the kids were coming by after school, they had to walk right past us, and we asked with a big smile on our faces if they wanted something to drink or needed a hat or gloves.

At first, they would look at us a little weird and were very cautious, but we introduced ourselves and shared that we wanted to start coming by each week with snacks and drinks; what did they think? To our excitement they said yes. It helped that some came by with their parents, so we got to talk to them also. Our first day was good. We had about fifteen kids show up, mostly elementary students, and one homeless. The kids were so excited, and we got a lot of questions. Why are you doing this, who are you, and are you coming back?

We knew we needed to be consistent, so we could start to build relationships with these kids. We planned to go out again in a week, and it would be exciting to see how many we would get to come by. To our excitement, the next week was also another nice day, and we were thrilled to have doubled the number of kids. I have found that when a youth knows you are for real, they start telling their friends, and it keeps going from there.

We got Rudy and his youth group to once again go down to Sumner to hang fliers and find any youth who may be wandering the streets of Sumner. It was the third week in December and the end of fall was going out with a bang; it was freezing. We ran into a couple of youth, and it was great that I had brought baggies of items: hats, gloves, scarves, and goodies just in case we ran into some needy youth or homeless. We were able to give one to a youth who had no gloves or hat, and it was so cool to see him down the street with the hat on. It was great to have Rudy's youth group come out and help us again. They had friends or people that they knew who were homeless, and this was their way of helping.

On Monday, once again we went down to the skate park, for the third time. As we set up, a young man who had been at the skate park skating came up to me and asked if we were the group that did barbecues. I told him it was a different ministry that no longer came down, but that we were starting an outreach here to feed the youth who come through. He then handed me five dollars and said, "It's not much, but I appreciate what you guys are doing."

Now, I honestly believe this could have been the only five dollars he had, but I believe he gave from his heart. He knew there was a need, and he wanted to help. The five dollars bought some more hot chocolate and cups, so it was very much appreciated and went to help us when we came back after the first of the year.

After our setup, the kids came running down the path that leads to the park. They were so excited to see us again, and this time we had twenty-six youth come by. We were all excited that more are coming by. A young man named Chris (he was 20) with spiked hair, a skateboard, pants that had been shortened, and two pairs of socks had a story to tell. He connected with Tamara, one of our amazing volunteers, a hairstylist, and they talked for about forty-five minutes. She was able to connect because of his hair since that is her job. God had told me *Love them where they're at*, and we were doing that. No judgment, just a smiling face, a *hello, how are you*, and food!

It was December, and I was so surprised at how many kids were without gloves. Thank goodness, one of our big donation items was gloves, so they got gloves, a hot chocolate, a granola bar, and a little book called *The Life Book*! *The Life Book* is the Book of John. One thing God told me at the beginning was that I was not to preach at the kids but just to love them. So we do that, but give them a book that I pray they will read. It is done up just for youth; it has pictures, and then next to the verses it has explanations of what the verse means, and that is written by a youth. I have wrapped them with Christmas wrap and candy. I heard a few kids call them the blessing book, and one even was in awe that it was from Jesus. I put an inscription in them "To you from Jesus."

We had two brothers, Michael and Timmy, come by. Michael was the youngest and extremely outgoing; he loved to talk to us and share his day with us. Timmy was very reserved and in middle school; it was his job to get his brother from elementary school and walk him home. It took some time, but Timmy finally came over. He would not take gloves at first but then he did. I almost forgot to give him his gift, but he left with new gloves, a gift, and a smile on his face.

Several high school boys came by. In fact, five on bikes went by; three stopped to get hot chocolate and gloves, went back, and talked to their friends, and then they came. They were all warming up to us, and seemed to enjoy talking, even the little ones. We handed out twenty-six little books about Jesus and life. We were starting to build relationships with the kids we were seeing, and that was a huge thing. Even in the short time of us going to the park, the kids are enjoying coming by to get some snacks. Kids are smart, and they take time to warm up to adults, especially ones they do not know.

We were going out again in one week. I was excited that my church was going to make up little bags of goodies and wanted to give them to us to hand out. They were paper sacks with pictures drawn on them; some are of the sun or maybe a flower, drawn by children in fifth and sixth grade. Inside were a granola bar, a juice, and crackers. We also had sixty-six more life books to hand out. If we could not hand them all out to the kids, we would be going to Fred Meyer and giving them to people as they leave the store—anything we can do to reach Sumner. On each of the books, we inscribed, "To someone special, from your friend Jesus and Mother 2 Many." This was a great way to have Sumner on board with what we are doing and just reaching our community.

Each time we have set up, two times now, geese have flown over us. In the book I'm reading, *Dreaming with God* by Bill Johnson, it talks about geese, that four geese represent the four corners and that they are protectors. The second time I had read about this, I was so excited, because this was a promise from God: *I am here and I am protecting you and the ones you are helping.* I know that when we go into Sumner or wherever God takes us, we have an army with us. He will not let any harm come to us, not a hair on our heads.

When we went out on December 22, it was great. We weren't sure how many youth we would see since it was Christmas break, but we were building relationships, so we hoped that some of the kids that lived nearby would stop and see us. Timmy and his three brothers showed up. Timmy ran to the end of the street, looked, and saw us there, and ran back to tell his brothers, "Hey, they are here," and ran back to see us. It was so wonderful to see this and when I said their names, I saw the biggest smiles come across their faces. Then he told us that they remembered we were coming out again, and he brought his older brother. Four brothers all got a book and goodies.

We had a lot of youth stop by this day. Many at first had a hard time trusting what we were doing; then one of their friends would come back and tell their friends it was OK. My niece even came by. She was with five friends; three came to us and got the hot chocolate, and the other two kept their distance, but as we kept going to the park, they soon realized we were OK. After our time with the kids, we headed over to Fred Meyer to hand out goodies and the rest of the life books. This was great. So many people were there since it was right before Christmas, and we gave all items out within fifteen minutes. I have not seen people smile as much as I did that night. This was a good day and night.

We went out again, and this time we met a young man that had seen our fliers and had just become homeless. As we were talking, he tried to tell me that he had no arrest warrants, but I stopped him.

GOING TO THE SKATE PARK

I did not want to know what he has done or has not done. He was homeless, and we were here to help and so thankful that he could get something to eat, gloves, and a hat. Doing what Jesus would do made my heart happy.

Steve and I had been talking about what happens when it rains, and we felt it would be good to get a canopy of some type. Well, as a new ministry, we did not have lots of money, and when we did have some money, it was a small amount and we would buy food items. So I told him, "As soon as we get some extra money, we will investigate this." Well, it was no more than two or three days when I went to my email page, and there was a donation from a friend—$500.00. My son-in-law had set up our web page with PayPal so people could check what we needed and then donate if they wanted. God was showing us that He would provide what we needed when we needed it; after all it was His ministry. God answered a prayer without us asking.

Now we could get a canopy for us to have when we go to the skate park, and that means we can be there rain or shine. And like Steve said, if we say we are going to be there every Monday, then we better be there. I think God was saying the same thing, and even if we live in Washington, we can make things work in the rain. God is so good, and we should be able to see it every single day. It may be little, it may be big, but He is there in everything.

After about three months, we had got enough donations to be able to buy a couple six-foot tables. This helped us to have a few more items to hand out to the youth. It was also brought to my attention that we needed to get insurance. At first, I thought, *Why do we need insurance?* Well, if a youth got burned drinking the hot chocolate, this could protect us. I never thought about that, so we stopped giving out hot chocolate until we had insurance. In fact, we found an insurance that took care of Christian ministries. We contacted them, found out how much it would cost, and then emailed a few people and asked if they could help us with the bill each month. To my excitement, we had five people say yes, which covered the entire amount of the insurance. God working once more.

We had been going to the skate park in Sumner now for eight months. God gave the skate park idea to me at the very beginning of M2M, but I was leading. I wanted things to happen so fast that I let things get out of control. I had talked to a woman named Pat right at the start of M2M, and she had said that we needed to go to skate parks, sit on a bench, bring water and granola bars, and maybe have some music, and the youth would come. Right there, God had planted that seed, and it needed time to grow. I needed to go a little slower and just wait on the Lord. I was not very good at waiting, but God has changed that. So, when all the other doors were closing, the skate park door was wide open. It has been amazing to see how the relationship with the youth had developed. We went from fifteen youth stopping by to sixty-two on the last day of school, June 2015. It has been amazing to see what God has been doing, and how He has provided for us, so wonderfully! I would think of something we needed, and I then get an email or a phone call that a person has just what we need. God is always providing for us.

During this time at the skate park, we had also been at two Project Homeless Connect events, and that had been great. We had so many toiletry donations. We wanted to find a way to help homeless, and this is what the Project Homeless Connect does. There were four of us that would get together to make little bags with toiletry items and hand them out. The second event was bigger, and we were able to pray with people. In fact, one of the people we prayed for went to the church of one of our volunteers. We were asked back to the event in October. God was using the season to change our hearts concerning the homeless. God was telling me, *Joann these are my children too, I need you to show them my love.*

June 2015 on a Monday, we decided to do hot dogs, and that was a hit. We had also started having chips, granola bars, cookies, fruit, juice, water, and even sandwiches. A local business in Sumner started to donate hot dogs to us so that we could continue to have them every Monday until the end of the school year. Then in September of the new school year, she told us she would continue to help us. She did this for a few years until we were able to get the hot dogs on our own. This was such a blessing, and the kids loved getting something hot and fun to eat. We had a mini barbecue that one of our team members bought for us, and that was how we cooked the hot dogs. It ran on propane, so it was very easy to work with.

It was the end of the school year, and we had asked the youth to tell us how they felt about us coming out each week to the skate park, and what they would think if we did not. We were told we would be missed if we did not come anymore. It was great to hear that they were glad we were there and they were able to eat. But the most touching was when a young man turned around as he left and said, "No one cares about the kids at the skate park. Thank you." Well, that touched each one of us that day, and you know what, it helped motivate us to keep going, doing what Jesus would do. We kept going to the skate park through the summer months, and it was great to see a smaller amount of kids, but they all knew we were not going away.

In fact, during the summer months, we were asked to go to two more parks, Puyallup and Allen Yorke. I was able to go to a Sumner Rotary meeting and share what I was doing at the skate park. To my amazement, most of the people there were very excited for what we were doing. The chief of Bonney Lake Police Department raised her hand at the end and said, "I want you to feed my kids." We started there right after school ended. Since the park is right by a lake, it was a great way to meet with youth during the summer and hand out water and snacks. This helped me call the chief of Puyallup and ask him if we could to the Puyallup skate park, and he was very happy to have us feed his youth also. Both parks ended at the end of summer, so then we could focus on Sumner since this was our main park and close to schools. Kids came there all year round, where at the other two parks they came only when it was nice outside.

Each park had different kids come by and that was so interesting, I had figured they would be pretty similar, but I was very wrong.

In Sumner the youth were very nice, but the older youth were very standoffish at first. It took time for them to really come to trust us, but after about six months, they were telling their friends about us and excited to see us each week. The age range here was eight to eighteen, and they usually got their food and headed home.

In Puyallup we saw mostly older youth, aged between fifteen and twenty-five. Most were pretty serious about skating, and were more than happy we came by. Some of the kids rode their bikes from Tacoma and Graham to go to this skate park; either direction is over ten miles. They would gather around us, sit on their bikes or skateboards and just sit and talk to us. It was really nice to go to this park and really get to know the youth that came by.

Allen Yorke had a great park with a lot of serious skaters here too, but a lot were younger. Age ranged here from about eight to twenty-five. The younger ones came with parents, which was great because we got to share with them about what we were doing, so here we met a lot more parents. They came to watch their kids skate and were giving them time of getting out of the house on a nice day. These youth usually didn't sit and talk. They liked to grab food and go back to the skate park and eat. We would have a few sit and talk, but they usually were the older youth.

All three parks had their personalities, but each was a joy to go to. We have always been so appreciated. Water was a hit on a hot day, and no drinking fountains were working.

God had really opened doors for us in just six months. The Thorndyke backpack program ended in June 2015, and was given back to the community of Tukwila, but Sumner, Puyallup, and Allen Yorke Skate parks all started up. God was letting us know we were doing exactly what He wanted. It was very exciting and very humbling to know God was entrusting us and the team of people we had come alongside us to love and feed His kids.

Now that we were feeding more, God showed up big-time when it came to us having snack items and bread to make sandwiches. This is how God worked on getting us the bread and snack items: I have a friend named Tess who was at a meeting, and Dennis—I will call him the bread man—came by. As they were talking, he shared about what he does and that he was looking for someone to come and get bread on a certain day. Tess told me that as soon as he shared this, my name came to her. When the meeting ended, she called and told me the story of meeting Dennis and then gave me his info.

I called Dennis, but he didn't answer, so I left him a message. When he called back, I understood why, Dennis is a very busy man, and helps so many other outreaches. He finally returned my call on a Monday. He said hello and asked me more about what we did. He wanted to know if I could use a lot of bread and said that he needed someone to commit to picking up bread each week on a Tuesday. I told him "Yes, that would be great. We could pick up each week." He then surprised me and asked if we could meet him that day in about thirty minutes and get some bread. With excitement I said yes.

When we showed up, we didn't know what to expect; we thought we might get twenty loaves of bread, and that would be it. Oh no, he gave us ten banana boxes full of bread and treats for the kids. Each banana box could hold ten loaves of bread. We had a lot of bread. He then told us we needed to get at least sixty banana boxes to pick up bread the next time we were there, which would be the next week.

I was a little overwhelmed by all this, but when we left with our ten boxes, I told Steve "OK, who can we bless with bread?" Since God had had me talk to a lot of people when we first started M2M, I knew some that might need some bread to give to their clients. By the time we ended this ministry the summer of 2018, our little bread ministry was huge. We went to four senior centers, an adult drop-in center, a community center, and a home for men with disabilities, and we gave to another person who gave to many people in need also. In just six months of starting this outreach, we had handed out over 50,000 bread items. God was giving us plenty to do, and we were loving it. It was amazing. I truly loved helping so many and spending time with so many people, from the littlest of kids to the seniors at the senior centers. It truly was a blessing to us.

As of September 2016, M2M was making over two hundred sandwiches each week and gave out about seventy hot dogs and forty bagels. I was spending a lot of time making sandwiches each week, so I was excited when three different groups offered to help make sandwiches for us.

Starting off the new school year, every Monday I had different groups of people bring us sandwiches for the kids. Sumner United Methodist started to make sandwiches twice a month, Banner Bank and Puyallup Kiwanis took another day, and a local business owner took the other day, so all four Mondays I had sandwiches. I no longer had to spend two to three hours making sandwiches, which was a huge blessing. Getting bread from Franz was a wonderful help, and really helped us to make sure the kids would always have sandwiches each week. We provided each team that made sandwiches the bread to make the sandwiches each week. Even after we stopped going to Franz, we financially were able to give them bread. Having someone make sandwiches was a huge help for me as we continued to grow.

When I had been at church the Sunday before we were blessed with bread, God had shown me a picture. I was standing in a field. The wind was blowing hard, my hair blowing all the way behind me, but I was standing firm, not moving. And that is when He said, "You stand strong even in the storm. Are you ready for something bigger?" The next day we got the call from the bread man. Yes, Lord, we are ready to go wherever you lead; we will follow!

God was doing wonderful things with our ministry. My prayer to him, was "*Father*, you have given us this wonderful opportunity. Lead us to where you want us to go." I posted on Facebook that we needed a freezer, and within a short time I got an email saying, "Hey, we have one, and you can have it." They had put it in their garage sale but did not sell it. God is so amazing; He knows before we do what we need, and He provides. We also received another call about a second freezer, so were now blessed with two. God knew what we needed, and He provided.

Our church has been a big help to us in the big items that would cost us a lot at a time of us just growing. We were able to use their fifteen-foot trailer to carry our bread in. As most of you know, it rains in Washington, and sometimes it rains a lot. We had a tarp to cover our banana boxes of bread, but no matter what, they were getting wet, so we asked to use one of the church's trailers. We were told yes! We were so excited, and our pastor told us, "This is great. We never use that trailer except once a year." Well, in two weeks they needed the trailer and then again a few weeks after that.

Hey, we totally understood, and that was good because we needed to have our own. We were getting ready to have our second fundraiser. Steve and I were talking, and I told him that we needed to find out how much a trailer costs so we can let our guests know at the fundraiser. Our friend Rudy, the youth pastor, worked for a car dealership, and when I called to ask to get a price for a trailer, he told me they had a trailer just like the one we were using from the church in their lot. I asked him to check the price, and he told me sure and he would get back to me. That was Wednesday morning. He called me that afternoon and said the owner of the dealership said we could have the trailer at his cost, $2500.00, if it was still up there.

Steve and I looked at each other and said, "Wow, let's go." We drove up to look at the trailer. At first we didn't see the trailer, and thought, *Oh no, it's gone.* But then we asked one of the salesmen, and he told us it was in the very back. Then he came with us and opened up the back door for us to look inside. It was a sixteen-foot trailer, it looked brand new, and the previous owner had put shelves in the front. It was perfect.

All we needed now was the cash to buy the trailer. After seeing the trailer, we told the salesman to please hold it, and he promised he would for twenty-four hours. I then hurriedly texted Rev. Pam and asked if her dad wanted to still help us, and if so, we needed $2500.00 to buy the trailer. In one of our earlier talks with Rev. Pam, she had told me that her dad wanted to help us in any way he could, so I was praying he still was feeling the same. I had spoken at a seniors luncheon that he attended before the skate park outreach started but knew we wanted to help homeless youth.

She called me Thursday morning and told me, "Dad will help, but he wants to buy you a house for the kids." Well, that was super exciting, but that was not where God was taking us right now. She then told me, "You need to go talk to him and share your heart." I told her we would love to and got his address and drove right out to his home.

Art is a man in his early nineties who has a heart to help those who are helping others. He is one of the kindest and humblest men I know. He invited us into his home, and we all sat in the living room, he in his favorite chair and Steve and I on his couch. We shared with him our hearts of where we felt God was taking us. We shared that in having a home for youth, we could help only four youth at a time, but we were helping hundreds at the skate park.

With his kind eyes, and sweet smile, Art totally agreed that we were going to help more youth at the skate park and was happy to help us. He then wrote us a check for $2800.00. I gave him a huge hug, and we said our good byes and headed to the bank, and then off to the dealership. By Thursday night we had our trailer. Within a few days, we even got to meet the wonderful man who had owned the trailer that night as he drove by our home. God will provide for all your needs, and He has done that with M2M, repeatedly. It is utterly amazing, and my heart is full and so touched by all He does for us.

June 2016 was our second fundraiser, and instead of a needing to raise funds for a trailer, we were able to put a huge decal on it. It has a big sun at the front and then Mother 2 Many, our Scripture, and our mission statement. What a blessing to have our own trailer, a godsend for sure.

Before the fundraiser I was running out of food for the youth, so I put out a request asking people for help. The people who gave did not come through a little bit; they came out huge. A business owner put this request on her Facebook page, and wow. Social media can be a huge way of getting the word out, and that has helped us a bunch. Our garage was full after this call for help.

God never puts you into something to fail, if you listen and do what He asks, things all fall into place, and that was what was happening. We were not just building relationships with the kids but with other outreaches that needed help. Exciting times. God was moving, and He was not going slowly.

Mondays at Sumner Skate Park were going well. We were feeding more youth every week. The youth were our best way to get the word out. They told their friends, and then their friends came, and so on. We now had a second freezer, and this was helping with us to be able to get more bread, hot dogs, and lunch meat, and not having to go to the store all the time. They all froze great. Our garage was getting full of all sorts of things for the ministry, so this was good! Our freezer was full every week and empty by the time to get more bread, so whenever I heard of a need, we helped.

As the summer wound down, we were seeing more homeless. In the last three weeks, we had seen ten homeless. They ranged from the age of nineteen to fifty-nine. We met those who wanted to stay on the streets and those who were trying to find any way to get off. It was sad, but I prayed that what we were doing was making their lives just a little easier for a week or so, and that we were becoming bolder praying for those in need or sharing a testimony to give hope.

This week before the end of school, we met a young man named Turner. When he came to us, he said, "Yes! I get to eat today."

I asked him, "What is going on that you just now get to eat?"

He told me with a sad look on his face that his mom had quit her job, and now they were going to get evicted because there was no more money. His mom couldn't pay the rent, and she couldn't buy food, and the food that they were getting from the food bank was very little. It looked like they were going to have to live in their car until she was able to find another job. He never told my why she quit, but from the way he sounded, something happened that made her want to get out of the work environment she was in.

This made me want to cry, as no child should go without food, no person should go without food. We were able to give him a food bag, and four sandwiches to hold him over for a few days. It was nice to have the backpacks for the homeless in the trailer, and by having them, I could also help Turner and his mom with a couple of them. The backpack program helped me know good items to put into these bags. Everything we have done so far has helped us to do what God called us to do at the skate park much better. The backpacks have nonperishable items—tuna and crackers, fruit cups, applesauce, Top Ramen, granola bars, Pop-Tarts and other single serving items—that can make up a meal.

Turner was so worried about taking the bag and didn't want to take from someone else in need, and I assured him it was OK. I got a hug and more than one thank you. This is why we were at the park, to help those in need, and over the years we have built a wonderful relationship with this young man. About six month after we met him, his mom did get back on her feet; she got a job, they got a nice apartment, and he did great in school. As of January 2022, he has graduated and is working to be an apprentice at a construction company. He has three cars. He loves coming to show us his newest one each time he finds a great deal. And I still get a hug and a thank you for still feeding him after he gets off work instead of school. A great relationship was built here, and we so enjoy seeing him.

The summer of 2016 was over, we had gone to two days a week at the Sumner Skate Park, Mondays and Wednesdays. There are a lot of low-income families in the area, and by us being at the park, it helped a lot of these families. Their kids got to eat an extra meal, and it helped with grocery costs for these families. We saw an average of fifty-plus people each time we were at the park. This was becoming much bigger than what we imagined, but God knew what was going to happen. He knew from the very beginning and knew that it would even get bigger.

I think some of my most favorite times were sitting and talking to the youth who came to see us. In front of our tables was a curb, and some of the kids would sit on the curb and eat, and as they did, they would talk to the team member that was close to them. I found this is a wonderful way to build relationships with each youth who came to see us. They each had a story. Some were good stories, like a young man we met who painted using spray paint. He did wonderful work, and he was very happy to share with us his beautiful artwork. In fact, one of my team bought him some paint so he could continue painting.

Another story of the people we saw was about a woman in her early to late sixties who is homeless. Her name was Patricia. She was about five feet tall, with messed up red hair. She always wore sweats, and her coat was usually dirty from sleeping in the woods. One thing was, she was very smart, but she was paranoid schizophrenic. She was a mother and grandmother. Her family had tried to get her off the streets, but had not be able to do so. One Wednesday, which was our hot dog day, she came by to get a hot dog, and she was able to sit in one of our chairs that were donated. She sat in the chair for over an hour, and then she went up to one of our team members and told him that sitting there made her feel like she was camping with family. That was one of the nicest things we had heard. She was so comfortable around us that she could call us family. That touched all our hearts. It let us all know we were making a difference, and we were doing what Jesus has called us to do.

Our mission is "To clothe all those that need to be clothed, to feed all those that need to be fed, to have a home for all those that need a home, to do what Jesus has called us to do."

God woke me up one morning and gave that to me. It goes along the lines of our Scripture, Matthew 25:35–40. It took some time before I truly understood all He had given me in that mission statement. We were clothing people, feeding people, *but what does the home mean, Lord?*

He told me this. "Joann, you are the home." He has given me a team that loves those kids. They have built relationships with the kids. They ask: How was your day? How was your weekend? What are you doing later? We were the safe place the kids could come to, and there was no judgment, only people who cared, family. God's pretty amazing!

As I wind down my story, I am reminded of how far we have come. God is not working slowly anymore, or at least to what we call slowly. He is moving faster; He is waking His people up. We are at war; we are warring with the enemy. We know who is going to win, but how many of us are going to get up, put our armor on and say yes to Him? How many are just going to sit on the sidelines and say, someone else will do it; I do not want to bother?

What Mother 2 Many is doing is a small part of what God has planned, He has a much bigger plan, a much bigger story, and I want to be a part of what He has, because no matter what, it will be an amazing story with an amazing outcome. Lives will be changed at the skate parks, and I cannot see myself anywhere but there with all the skaters that I have come to love so dearly.

God has opened doors that only He could open. M2M has grown. As of 2019, we are in Enumclaw, Buckley, Bonney Lake, Sumner, Puyallup, Orting, Roy, Yelm, and Eatonville, and we help the Bethel School district. M2M feeds over five hundred people each week. We sold our home of twenty-seven years, and that was a total God thing—now we have a four-car garage for our outreach. The bread outreach was also for a season, and we did that for three years, but now our main focus is on the skate parks and feeding the youth. We have been in three newspapers, on the news, and on a TV program. We have met so many people, so many amazing youths and adults.

At a board meeting, one of the board members wanted to make sure that when the kids left us, they would have something to encourage them. She came up with the idea of having bands made up that said these especially important words: I MATTER! The band has made a difference in many lives.

We had a lady come by named Amanda, who got some food for her neighbor, Nicole, who had been really feeling down. Nicole had been overwhelmed with having three autistic children, and she was a single mom. Amanda's son took an extra band to take to Nicole. When Amanda got to the door to give the food and band to Nicole, little did she know that Nicole was about to take her own life. When she came to the door, and they gave her the food and band, she looked at that band and said, "'I Matter.' . . . I matter!" The cool thing about that band, it glowed in the dark, so even at night Nicole could look at that band and say, "I matter." The band and the words on the band saved her life.

Only God could do that, and since those words came from Him, they did what they were meant to do, to let someone know they mattered. I see Nicole all the time, and she is doing great; she just got married. On another occasion, I had a young man open the door for me to go into the mall. I then grabbed a band and told him that if he didn't want it, maybe he could share it with someone else. He then replied, "No, I need to know I matter too." Those bands are so little, but they mean a lot to so many. I have included the words *You are not forgotten* on the other side. Our youth need to know that more than ever right now. Every life matters!

As my journey continues, God reminds me always that He is never far away, and that He will always be our provider. There were so many times when I would need something, and I would not even have to ask. God would provide. I was asked to speak at a meeting for the seniors at Sumner United Methodist Church. Before I left to go down to the church, I looked at the supply of peanut butter and thought, *I need to put a post out asking for some.* I went to the meeting, shared with them our needs, and when I was finished, I went out to my car and listened to my voice mail. My friend from Calvary Community Church had left a message. "Hey are you still feeding the youth at the skate park? If so, I have peanut butter for you." I called her and then went to pick up the peanut butter and got forty-five forty-ounce jars of peanut butter. I did a happy dance, that was so cool. Then I shared this with my friend and told her, "I should not have to worry about peanut butter for a while," and she said, "Well, maybe you will be making more sandwiches." I love my friends; they always bring the better side of things into perspective. And yes, we were about to make a lot of sandwiches.

Dear Father, thank you for your provision, for the wonderful people you bring into our lives. Thank you for asking me to be your hands and feet. In Jesus's name, amen.

CHAPTER 16

Seeing God's Hand in Everything We Have Done

*The Lord bless you and keep you; the Lord make his
face shine on you and be gracious to you; the Lord
turn his face toward you and give you peace.*

Numbers 6:24–26

As I close my story, I see God's hand in everything. God was working much faster once He had shifted us into the right spot we were meant to be. Even in the parts that I was off track, He was teaching me how to not give up even when nothing seemed to be going smoothly. He was teaching me to keep moving forward, to learn from my mistakes, and what to take from those mistakes, and how to turn those mistakes into successes. Additionally, He was teaching me about the excitement from the successes because more would come.

I learned that God will always encourage, and you may never know who or what He may use to do that encouraging. We did a bread outreach for a few years. One day during the summer of 2016, we were meeting someone to give them bread. It was hot outside for Washington. I was waiting at the skate park and had opened the back of the trailer, when all of a sudden, a young man in his early twenties appeared. His brown hair was long, kind of greasy, like a rocker, an angel rocker. His guitar caught my eye because I had never seen anyone with a guitar at the skate park before. I was mesmerized in a way, and as he walked by, I asked him if he would like some water or a snack?

He told me that he would like a water. I asked what he was doing. He was headed to a friend's house to play his guitar. As I was getting his water, he said, "I just want you to know that you are making a difference here."

I turned and said, "Sometimes I wonder if we are."

Then without hesitation, he said, "You are making a difference!"

I teared up hearing those words. We had been going to the park for eighteen months, and I wasn't sure if we were making a difference, and his words touched my heart. As I watched him walk away, I said, "I think you're an angel."

Turning, he smiled this amazing smile at me and continued on his way.

His words made me cry because it was something that I needed to hear. It made me happy and joyful that he would encourage me like that. It is neat how God can use anyone to get His point across. I have never seen the man with the guitar again. To this day I know he was sent by God to let me know that we were making a difference. He was an angel in rocker fashion.

When God told us we were to be seed planters at the beginning of our journey, I had forgotten that he told me that, but then I was reminded again. God always brings someone to confirm what He has said.

He did that with a young man who came to us in the spring of 2019. The young man who painted with spray paint came back to see us. We had not seen him in close to two years. He came up to me and asked, "Do you remember me?" with a big smile on his face.

I said with a smile that I did.

We got to talk for a while, and then he shared, "I wanted to let you know that you all showed me Jesus. My family didn't go to church and never talked about God, but because of your kindness and showing the community God's kindness, you showed me Jesus."

I stood there with tears in my eyes, thinking that was one of the kindest things I have heard in a long time.

He told me he was going someplace that he was able to do activities, and they had Bible studies. He was being watered, when we had planted the seed. He talked with us the whole hour that we were at the park, and then we said our goodbyes, I haven't seen him since. but I knew that he would be OK.

Later that evening I also received a nice card from a friend:

> You have a heart for the broken; the people most will walk past without a thought. I've seen the compassion and the love you bring to the children, and I also know that you won't tolerate injustice. I love the way you show God to others.

Yes, show God to others. That is what He wanted us to do, and we were doing just that.

Another time in the spring of 2017 at a women's retreat, I had gone outside. The resort was surrounded by trees. I sat on a bench and admired the beauty surrounding me. As I did so, God said to me, "Do you see all those trees? Those are all the youth whom M2M will help."

I replied, "God, there are millions of trees."

"Yes, there are. You will plant a seed, and from there it will keep going and never stop."

My eyes filled with tears, God was revealing more to me about M2M, and the timing was His timing. He filled my heart with awe of what God would be doing with M2M. And then I was reminded that from those trees there are millions of seeds. God has a plan for our lives, and no matter what, they are important plans. You may think that you cannot do whatever you are doing, and that is fine. He will use you where you can help, donate food, make hats, invest financially, set up a web page, do taxes, and so on. God can use you. You just have to say, *Yes, Lord, I am willing. Where do you want me to go?*

We were told it would take us over eight years to build our ministry. In five years, our ministry had grown more than we could have ever imagined. In just one afternoon, Sumner alone has seen up to 250 people, and 95 percent are youth. Are we a success? I think so, but only because God has made it that way. We have built some great relationships with the community, the youth, and the families.

At the very beginning God had told me that we would help homeless teens, and one day on one of my drives, I asked, "Lord, You told me homeless teens, I know we have helped some, but not very many."

His reply, "Joann, just because a teen has a home, doesn't mean they are not homeless."

That hit me like a brick. That is who we are helping: those who have a home but are truly homeless. God revealed to me what homelessness is to Him, and these were the youth who were truly forgotten. People do not think of a youth being homeless when they have a home, but when their parents are not involved, they are homeless.

At the start of 2020 we were seeing so many youth. At the Sumner Skate Park we saw almost 250 people in one day; our numbers were growing, and then COVID-19 hit. The parks are closed, and I wonder what the Lord would have us do now. Well, we are to keep feeding the kids, but now we are to do things a bit differently. Another short detour. Although the parks were closed, other outreaches needed our help.

I even got an email from a church organization that was feeding more kids than normal. They wondered if we could help with food items for their backpack program. Then we also heard from a school district that visits family homes and drops off food, who need help with another backpack program. And then a family center in a nearby town is in real need. So instead of skate parks, we take food to organizations who help the youth and their families.

Our work is not done just because there was a bump in the road. It just meant we needed to take another road for a while. For thirty days we weren't able to go to the parks. Soon we were back at Sumner and Yelm and Allen Yorke in the summer, and also doing the other places who had asked for help.

We were excited to get to go to three of our regular parks, but it was different at our main park in Sumner. Once school started, the kids were all learning from home, so that meant we were not seeing the regular number of kids coming by. Since they do not have to walk by us at the park to get home, we only go out when it is not raining. God taught me something important. It does not matter how many you see, but *who* you see.

We know that this is just another bump, or even a small detour, but we know that God is working. In this time, we have built some great relationships with people we probably would not have met before, and that is wonderful. God never takes you down the wrong path if you listen to Him.

After almost eight years since M2M started, I think my ears are pretty cleaned out, and that is good. I still love doing what we do. I love seeing the kids run to see us and getting smiles and even hugs. My heart is happy. God has given me the best gift ever, serving His kids. There are no regrets, only thankfulness. To have my heavenly Father trust me with His most precious gifts, our youth, is simply amazing, and it is something I hope I do until He takes me home.

Dear heavenly Father, please guide us, direct us, and give us wisdom in what You are calling us to do. Let us not fear if there is a detour but take joy in knowing that You trust us to do great things. Thank You, Father, for trusting us with Your kids. In Jesus's Name. Amen.

CHAPTER 17

Feed Them and They Will Come, Doing What I Do

"'For I was hungry and you gave me something to eat, I was thirsty and you gave me something to drink, I was a stranger and you invited me in, I needed clothes and you clothed me, I was sick and you looked after me, I was in prison and you came to visit me.'

"Then the righteous will answer him, 'Lord, when did we see you hungry and feed you, or thirsty and give you something to drink? When did we see you a stranger and invite you in, or needing clothes and clothe you? When did we see you sick or in prison and go to visit you?'

"The King will reply, 'Truly I tell you, whatever you did for one of the least of these brothers and sisters of mine, you did for me.'"

—Jesus, in Matthew 25:35–40

Feed them and they will come.

People want to do something, but they need a place to start, and a person to start it.

God had me start a skate park outreach, something I knew nothing about. He first gave me the seed, our name, to get started, and then He brought me the teachers. In all that time He also worked on me. He took away hurts and gave me a heart to love those who seem to be forgotten and alone.

It is hard to realize how many youths feel that they do not matter to anyone. There are far too many. God has really spoken to me about that little word *matter*. It is a word that breaks my heart, because so many youths and even adults think they do not matter. M2M is focused on making our young people know that they matter, and by your stepping out and reading this book, perhaps you sense the youth need to know too. This book will help you to do what we do, loving our youth right where they are at, because our youth need to have more people step out and show the love of Jesus. I hope that you, too, will decide to go to your skate park, set up a table, give out snacks, and show the youth in your community that they are not forgotten. My heart breaks for the young people of today, and I pray that God will break your heart too. But I hope that your heart does not stay broken but be molded into a tender, loving heart for our youth.

> *Remember you do not have to know everything about what you are doing. God takes the unqualified and qualifies them.*

When you are called into a ministry, the first thing that is so important is to get confirmation. Have people pray with you and for you. Make sure you have the support of your spouse and your family; this will make your life much easier. Remember you do not have to know everything about what you are doing. God takes the unqualified and qualifies them. Since I am one of the few who work with teens, I will have people call and talk to me about youth. I tell them that God qualified me, He is your teacher. It can be scary stepping out and saying yes, and working with youth can be even scarier. Being consistent is so important, and knowing when not to cross the line is important too.

God showed me the sweetest picture: He was holding my heart. He wanted to make sure I knew that He wouldn't let me get hurt, and my heart wouldn't be broken, as long as I did my part. Not crossing the line has helped me. Do not let yourself get caught up in everything. You can't fix everyone; that is God's job. You are to be there for them and lend a listening ear, a supportive smile, and words of encouragement. For the most part, the youth we work with are so sweet and always very thankful for what we do. Yet you will run into those who want to strike back, which you can't take personally. Others will abuse your caring spirit; just remember they have been hurt too. God will protect you!

Once you know what you are called to do, get others to surround you who are like-minded, and remember when God gives you people who want to help, let them help. I'm terrible about that, but one day God told me, "Joann, I have given you volunteers to help. Now let them help." Now, I stay behind and stock items while letting my team feed the youth. When you have volunteers, if you are working with youth, you need to do background checks on them. This is free through the state patrol in some states.

Now it will depend on what you are doing, but becoming a 501c3 is important. You can have your church be an umbrella to start off with, but you will need to be your own. Do not let that scare you as it did me. God will bring you someone to help.

We had a plan to start at the park. We got a table, hot chocolate, gloves, hats, and granola bars to start with. You do not have to start big. God wants to provide for you and His kids. Remember those two words: *His kids*. As you grow, He will bring in the means for you to grow. Do not get discouraged, it takes time, and all will fall into place. Remember your journey is like a puzzle, some are small some are big, and they all need to fall into place at just the right time, and they must go into the right spot to work.

It is also so important to be welcomed into the place you are going. M2M is mainly in small towns or cities. Larger cities have a lot of red tape to go through, and that costs a lot of money. We also start with the police chief to get permission to go to the park or skate park. If they cannot give that OK, it will go to the mayor and city council, and we have always been welcomed. Doing things right is always a good thing, and being welcomed into a place is the right first step.

Spend a lot of time in prayer. Prayer is so important; it will help you to stay strong, and hopefully focused. There will be bumps, but that is OK; that is how we learn. You will have people with you for a season, some for the whole time, and that is OK. Everything and everyone have a purpose in what you are doing. Also, God will bring people into your life that you have not seen for years and God will use them to help you with your cause.

God wants you to succeed, and that is so important to remember. If He called you to do something, He knows you can do it, He does not want you to fail. So do not give up. I did not, and look what happened. God is your biggest cheerleader.

Social media is a good way to ask for help, or if you are a letter writer, sending notes to your friends and family sharing what you are doing helps you get started. If you are going to feed youth, talk to your local food bank. They always have extra items, and they love to help you because in the long run you are helping them too. Talk to your church, share your needs, ask if you can have a bin to start collecting items. Do not get discouraged if some are not on board with what you are doing. God will open other doors to bring help. But you must make the first step in getting what you need. Share with women's groups; they love to help when it comes to youth. There are always those who want to help by making hats and scarves, and they also like to do food drives. Great way to get started, and it will help to build your confidence in knowing there are people out there wanting to help.

I want to share one last story, and I hope it touches your heart as much as it touched mine.

Tonight Steve and I stopped at Safeway to buy some groceries. As we were walking down an aisle, I saw a young man who was homeless, and as he walked, the sole of his shoe flopped. My heart all of a sudden became very sad for the young man in his twenties with shoulder-length black hair with a trace of gray. We passed him, and he made sure he was out of our way and wouldn't make eye contact.

We continued our shopping, and I then knew God was asking me to buy his groceries. So when I went up to the cashier, I asked if he had come up to buy his groceries. The store was empty, and the cashier, who knew him, said she hadn't seen him yet. I was worried that maybe he had walked out, but she assured me he hadn't, that he was good about paying. She suggested a gift card, and went and got me one.

I paid for the card, and looked one more time down the aisle. He once again moved aside, looking down.

As I looked at his basket, I noticed he was being very mindful of what he was buying, and he had cash in his hand. I went up to him and gave him the card, saying, "This is for you. Be blessed."

I couldn't hear what he said, but he was very surprised. Steve said he just looked at the card like he didn't believe it was real.

With this story I wanted you to see the person not as a homeless man but as a human. He had been truly beaten down, you could tell that, and by his actions, he wasn't looking for handouts. He was truly thankful that he would be able to eat for a few days.

God saw him, and through me, God showed him that he wasn't forgotten. Everyone matters to God, and it is nice when He uses us to let them know that!

God let me see the young man again about a month later. Steve and I were driving home from the Yelm skate park and there he was walking toward Safeway. He was wearing a pair of new shoes.

God is so good. I wouldn't have done something like that nine years ago, but now I won't hesitate. God changed my heart.

In ending my story, I pray that God will open your eyes and ears to what He has for you. That you will say yes with excitement and anticipation for what He has for you. That you will not fear the unknown but go confidently knowing that God is with you and for you. And most of all, you are so loved by a heavenly Father who chose you before you were born to be a part of something wonderful. Saying yes will be the best thing you have ever done. Now go get them; they are waiting!

"Then he said to his disciples, 'The harvest is plentiful, but the workers are few'" (Matthew 9:37).

Dear Father, we ask for guidance, we ask for eyes to be open, and we ask that You work in each of us to become the person You destined us to be. Let us not fear the unknown, for You are with us. Let us do what You have called us to do and let us do it well. In Jesus's name, amen.

CPSIA information can be obtained
at www.ICGtesting.com
Printed in the USA
JSHW020327060223
37325JS00002B/144